# ULTIMATE
# FANTASTIC
# FOUR

# INHUMAN

# ULTIMATE FANTASTIC FOUR

## INHUMAN

writers
**MIKE CAREY (THINK TANK) & MARK MILLAR (INHUMAN)**
pencils
**JAE LEE**
colors
**JUNE CHUNG**

letters
**CHRIS ELIOPOULOS**
covers
**BRYAN HITCH & LAURA MARTIN; JAE LEE & JUNE CHUNG;
GREG LAND, MATT RYAN & JUSTIN PONSOR**
assistant editors
**JOHN BARBER & NICOLE WILEY**
editor
**RALPH MACCHIO**

collection editor
**JENNIFER GRÜNWALD**
assistant editor
**MICHAEL SHORT**
senior editor, special projects
**JEFF YOUNGQUIST**
director of sales
**DAVID GABRIEL**
production
**JERRON QUALITY COLOR
& JERRY KALINOWSKI**
creative director
**TOM MARVELLI**

editor in chief
**JOE QUESADA**
publisher
**DAN BUCKLEY**

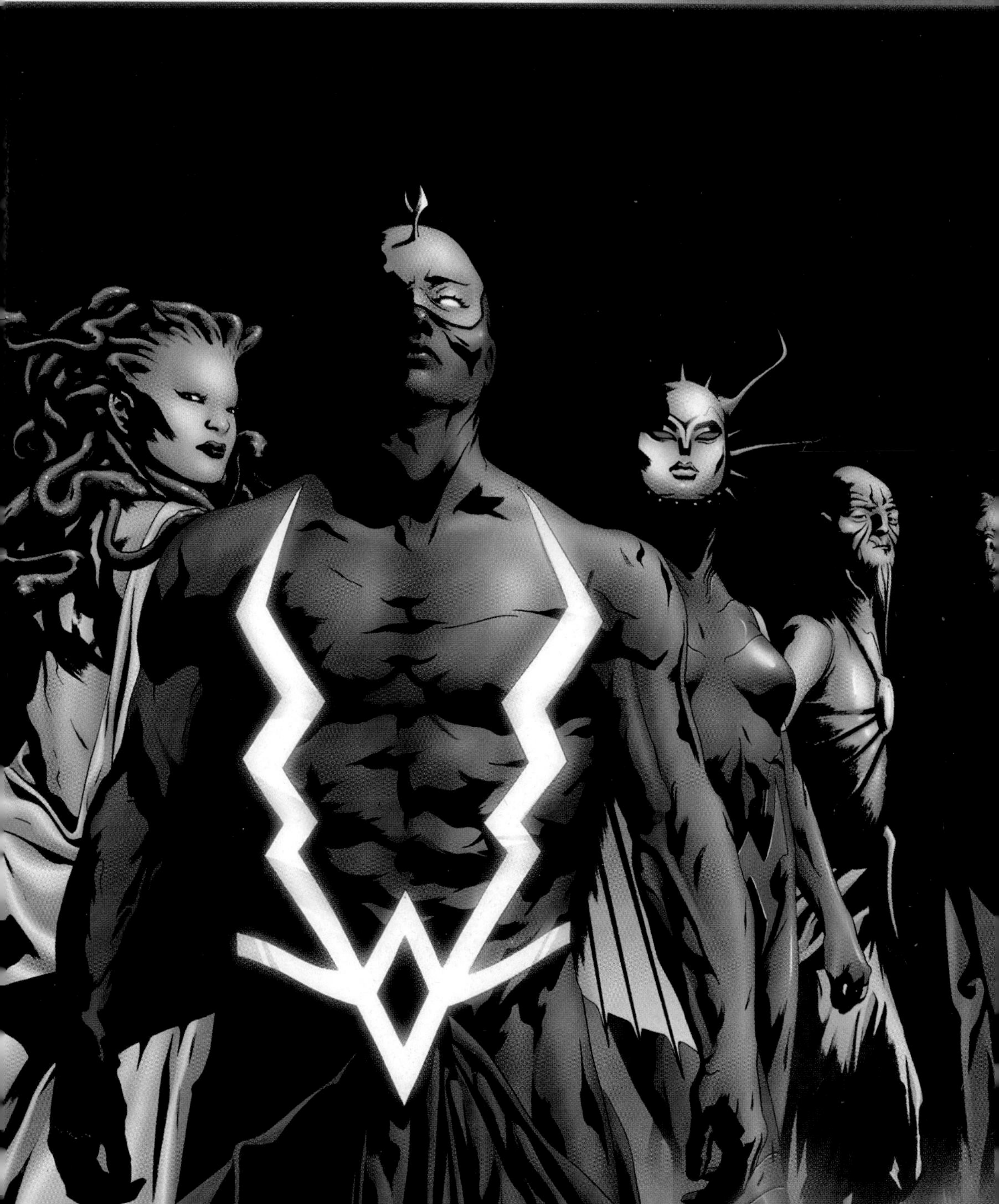

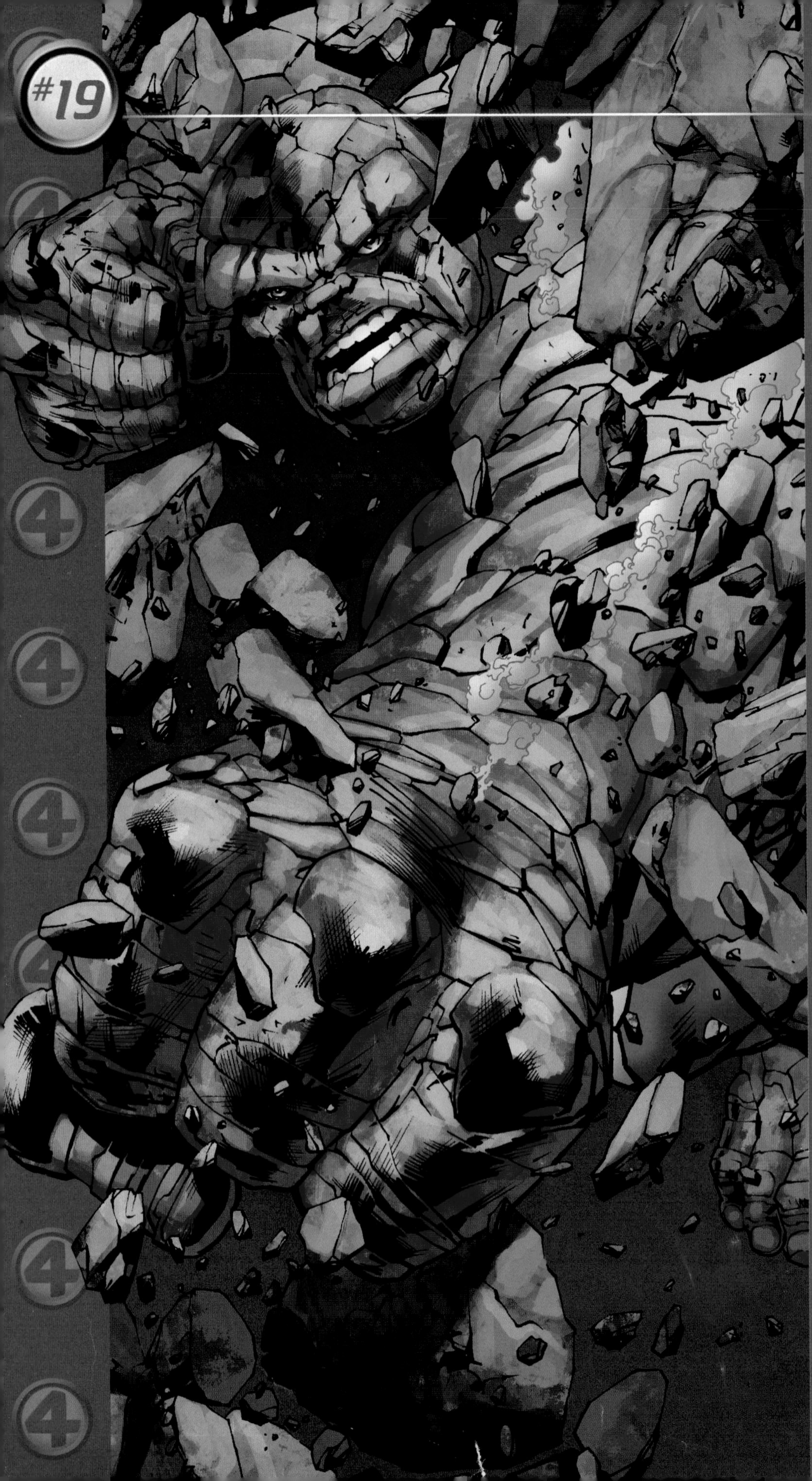
#19

# PREVIOUSLY IN ULTIMATE FANTASTIC FOUR:

Reed Richards, handpicked to join the Baxter Building think tank of young geniuses, spent his youth developing a teleport system that transported solid matter into a parallel universe called the N-Zone. Its first full-scale test was witnessed by Reed, fellow think tank members Sue Storm, Sue's younger brother Johnny, and Reed's childhood friend Ben Grimm.

There was an accident. The quartet's genetic structures were scrambled and recombined in a fantastically strange way. Reed's body stretches and flows like water. Ben looks like a thing carved from desert rock. Sue can become invisible. Johnny generates flame. The team's existence remained a closely guarded secret.

Reed, Sue, Ben, and Johnny become the first people to explore the N-Zone, travelling there in the modified space shuttle Awesome. After an inter-dimensional battle with a malevolent creature called Nihil, the FF manage to save the Earth from an alien invasion—in the streets of Las Vegas. The team returns to the Baxter Building, their existence now a matter of public record.

# THINK TANK

## PART 1 OF 2

They're coming

Altitude fifteen hundred feet vector 76 degrees three minutes from West velocity 102 mph acceleration zero steady as she flies they're coming

ON  OFF  1  2  3  4

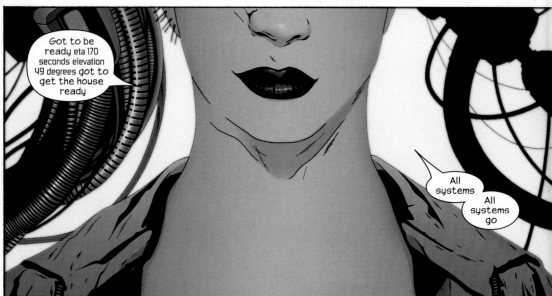

Got to be ready eta 170 seconds elevation 49 degrees got to get the house ready

All systems

All systems go

"Oh Richards Richards Reed Reed read-only Richards"

"I can't tell you how much *seratonin* .002 norepinephrine .00015--"

"--I'm looking forward to this"

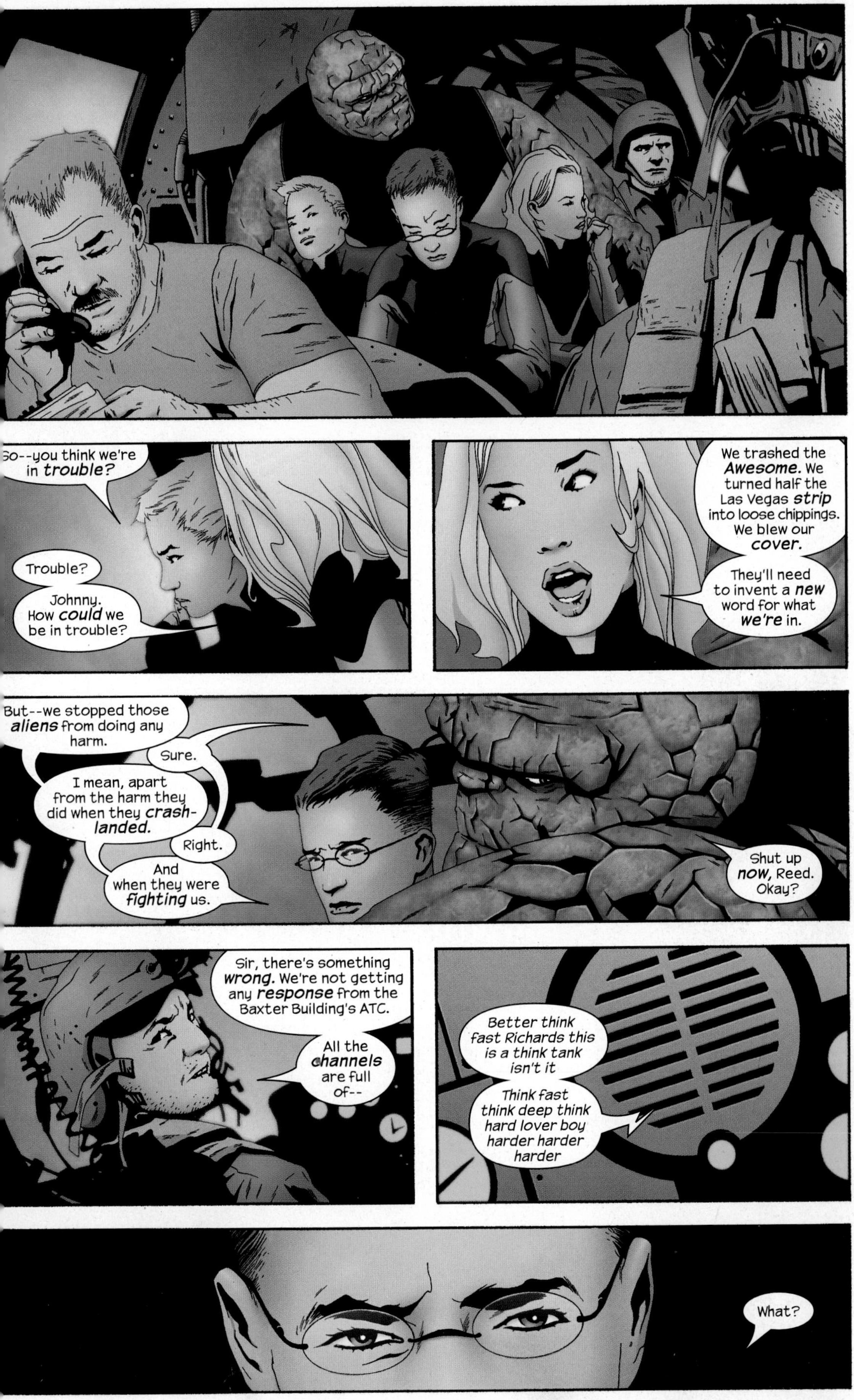

So--you think we're in trouble?
Trouble?
Johnny. How could we be in trouble?
We trashed the Awesome. We turned half the Las Vegas strip into loose chippings. We blew our cover.
They'll need to invent a new word for what we're in.
But--we stopped those aliens from doing any harm.
Sure.
I mean, apart from the harm they did when they crash-landed.
Right.
And when they were fighting us.
Shut up now, Reed. Okay?
Sir, there's something wrong. We're not getting any response from the Baxter Building's ATC.
All the channels are full of--
Better think fast Richards this is a think tank isn't it
Think fast think deep think hard lover boy harder harder harder
What?

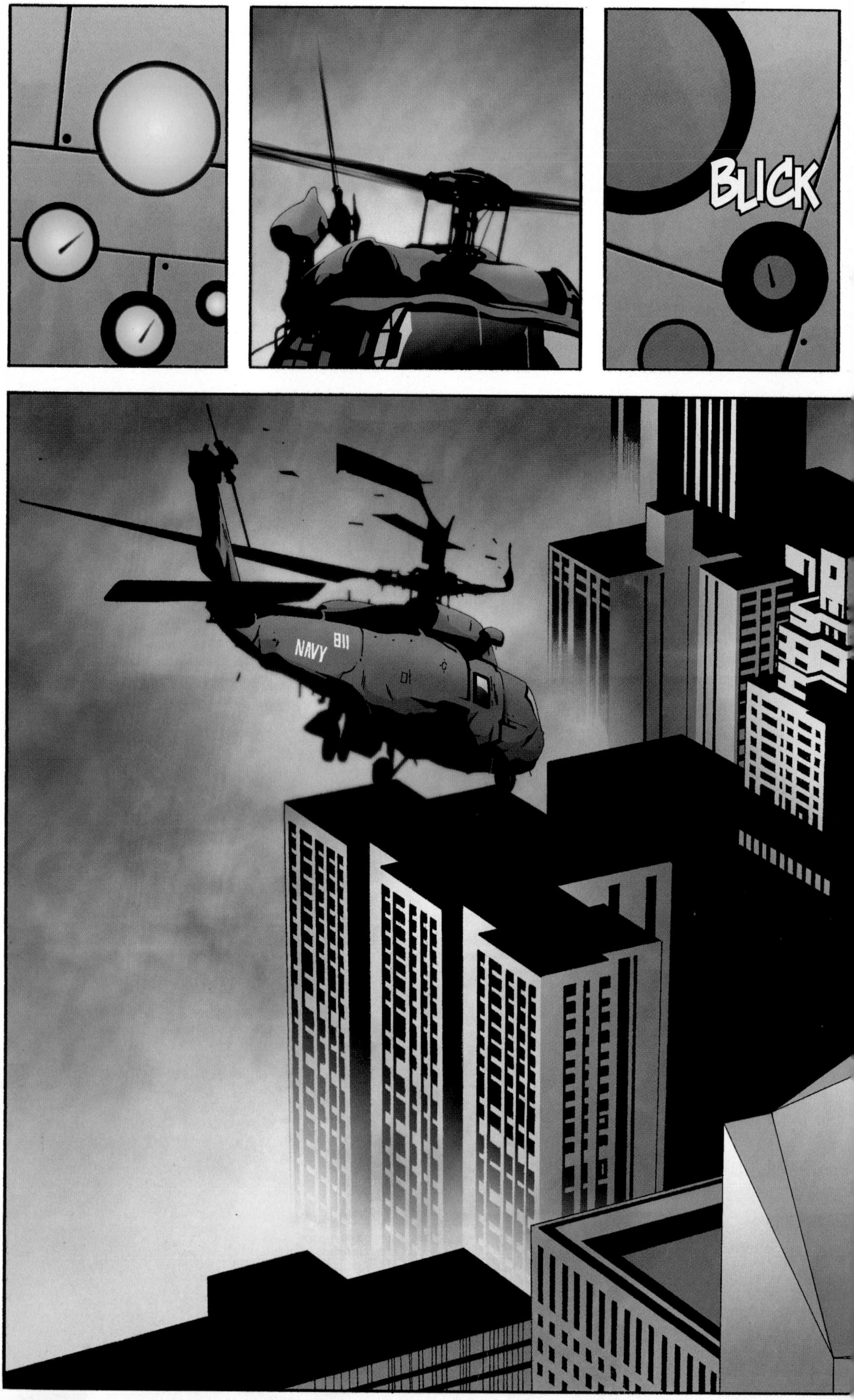
BLICK
NAVY

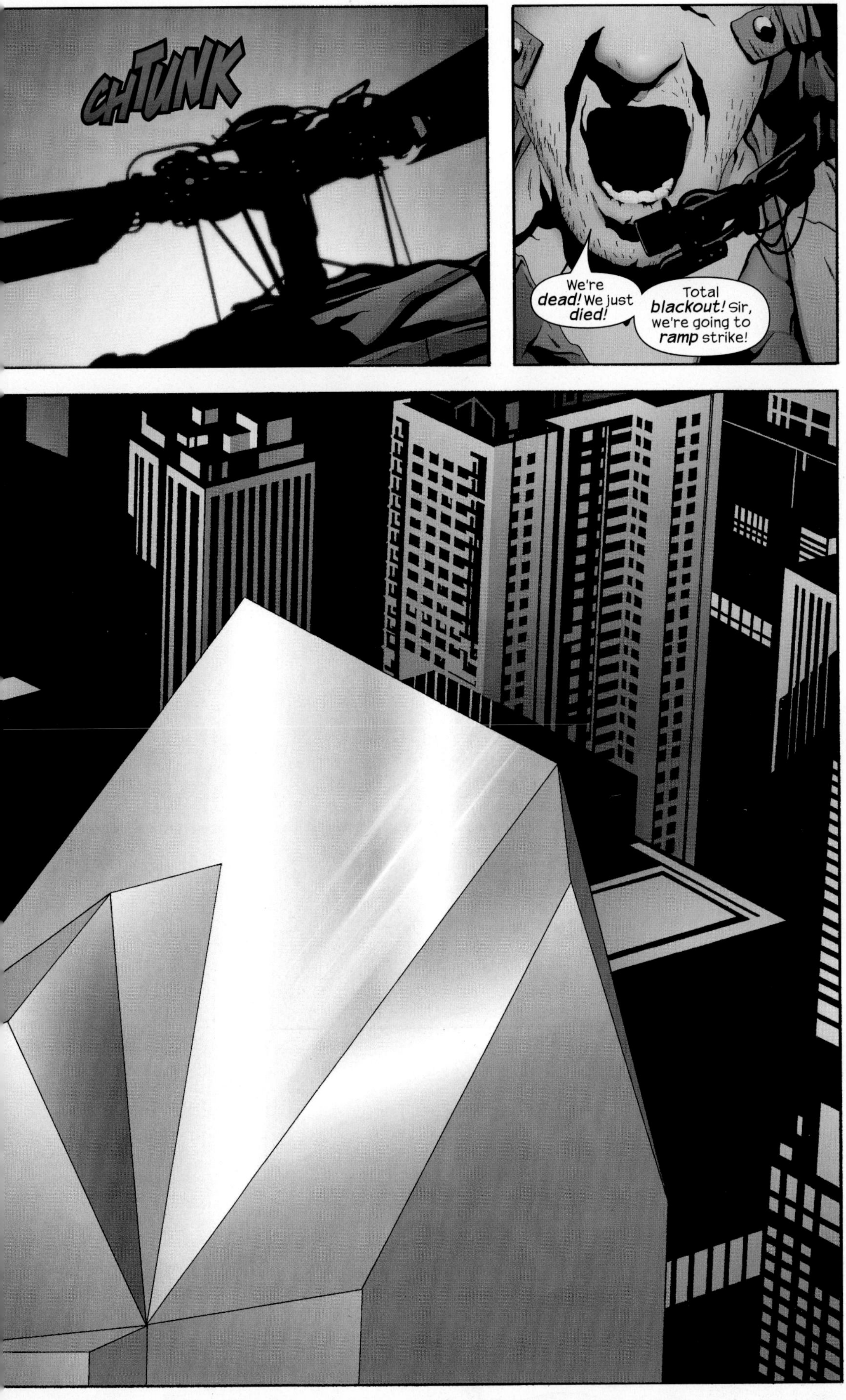
CHTUNK
We're dead! We just died!
Total blackout! Sir, we're going to ramp strike!

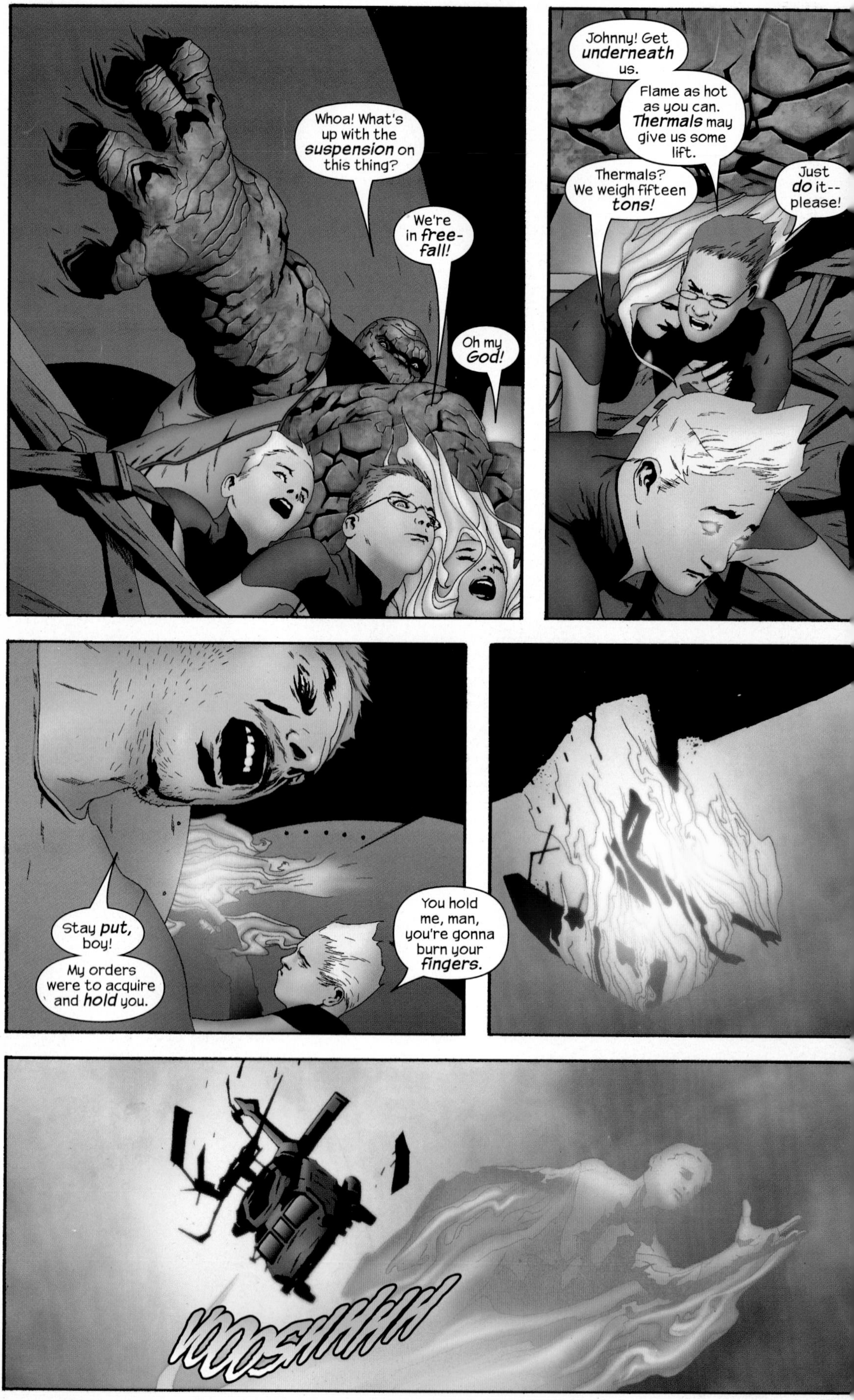
Whoa! What's up with the suspension on this thing?
We're in free-fall!
Oh my God!
Johnny! Get underneath us.
Flame as hot as you can. Thermals may give us some lift.
Thermals? We weigh fifteen tons!
Just do it-- please!
Stay put, boy!
My orders were to acquire and hold you.
You hold me, man, you're gonna burn your fingers.
VOOOSHHHHH

Reed, Johnny's *right.* Thermals won't lift something this *heavy!*

Of *course* not. But they may *slow* it.

Ow! Hot!

And I'm going to slow it some *more!*

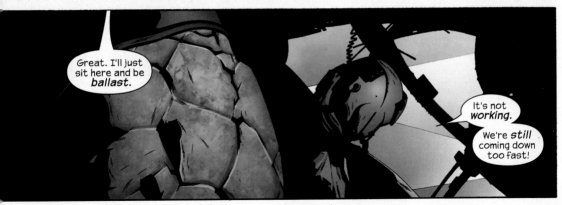

Great. I'll just sit here and be *ballast.*

It's not *working.*

We're *still* coming down too fast!

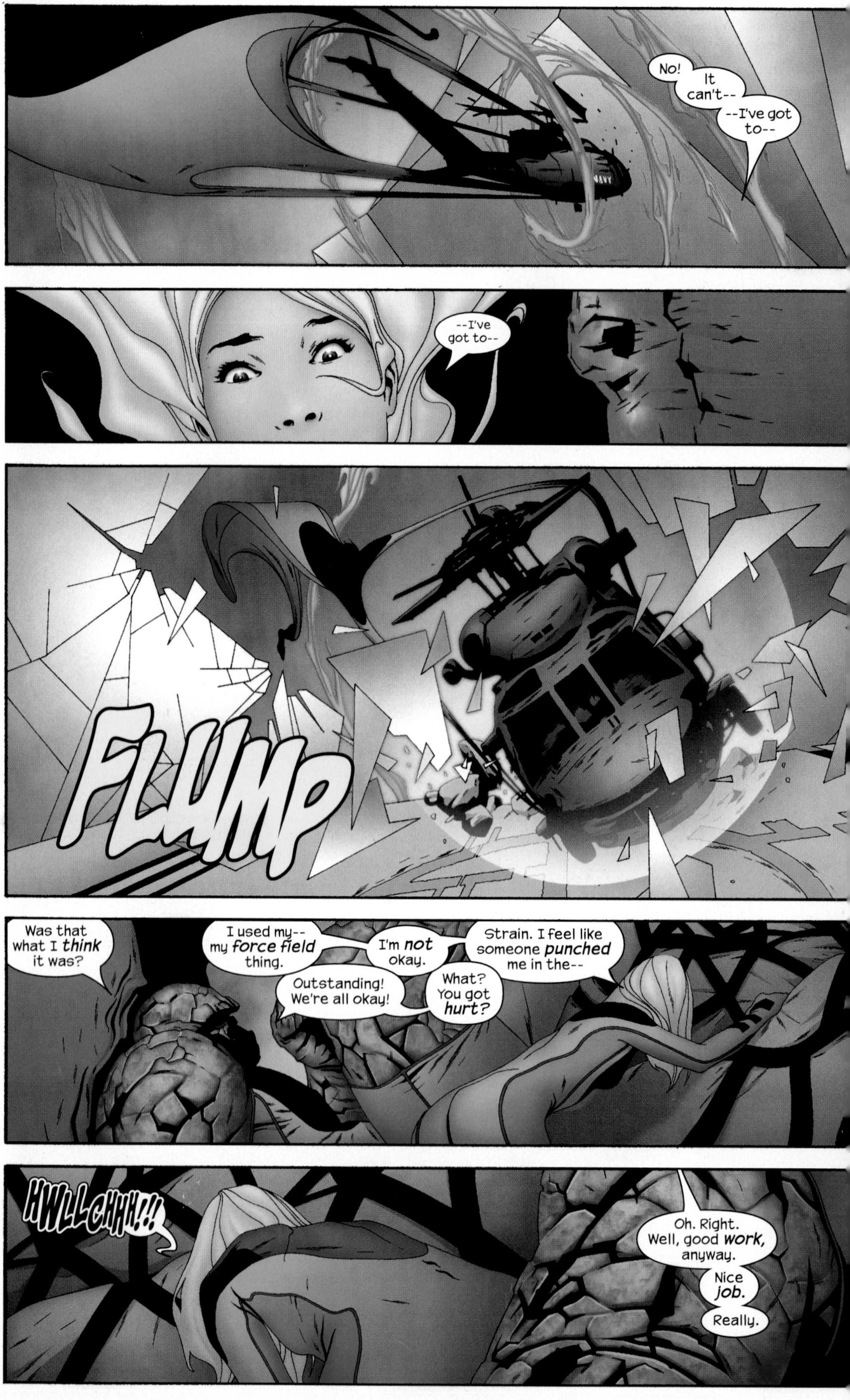
No!
It can't--
--I've got to--
--I've got to--
FLUMP
Was that what I *think* it was?
I used my-- my *force field* thing.
Outstanding! We're all okay!
I'm *not* okay.
What? You got *hurt?*
Strain. I feel like someone *punched* me in the--
HWLLCHHH!!
Oh. Right. Well, good *work,* anyway.
Nice *job.*
Really.

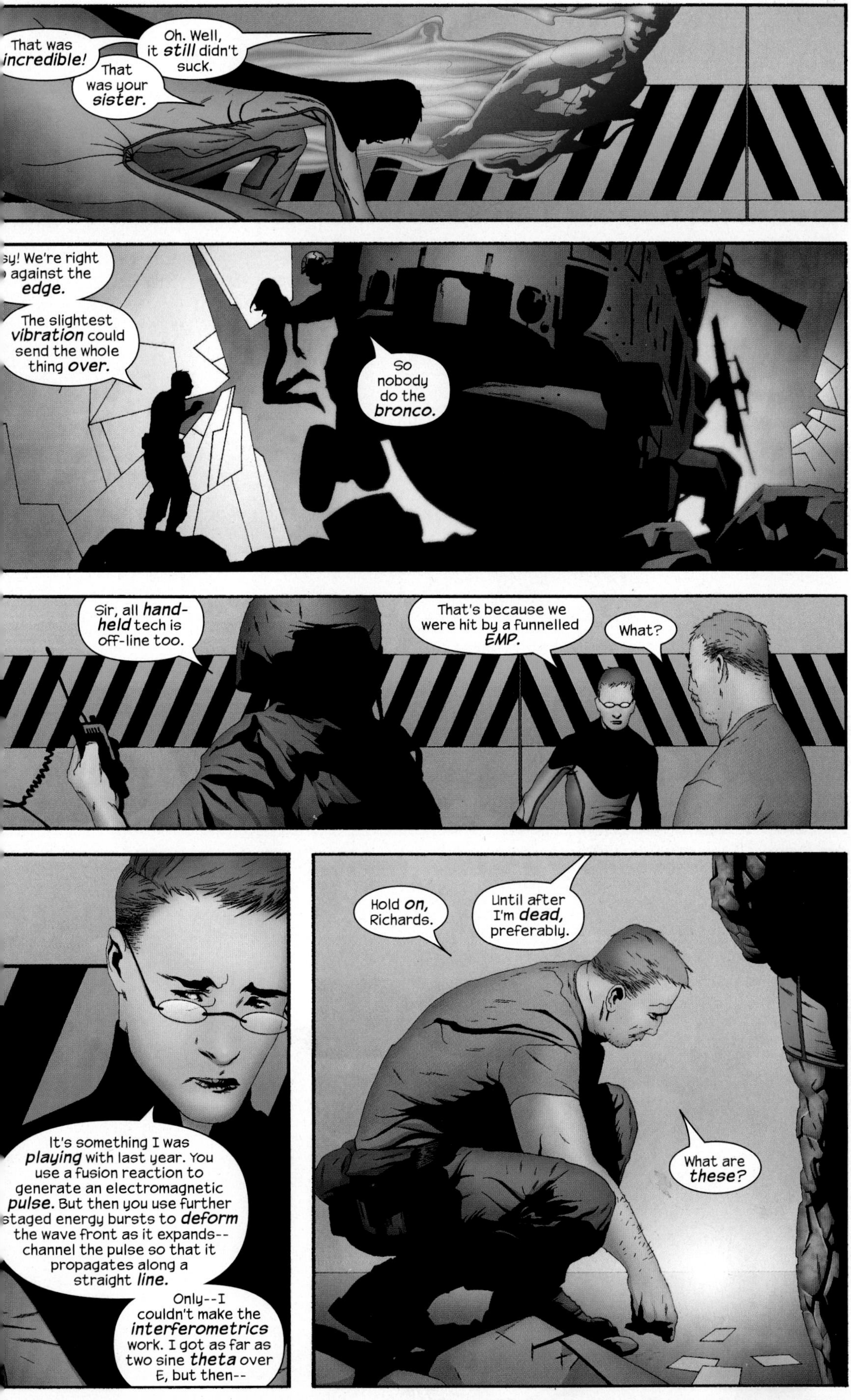

That was incredible!
That was your sister.
Oh. Well, it still didn't suck.
sy! We're right against the edge.
The slightest vibration could send the whole thing over.
So nobody do the bronco.
Sir, all hand-held tech is off-line too.
That's because we were hit by a funnelled EMP.
What?
It's something I was playing with last year. You use a fusion reaction to generate an electromagnetic pulse. But then you use further staged energy bursts to deform the wave front as it expands--channel the pulse so that it propagates along a straight line.
Only--I couldn't make the interferometrics work. I got as far as two sine theta over E, but then--
Hold on, Richards.
Until after I'm dead, preferably.
What are these?

I.D. cards, sir. *Ours.* Drummond... Green...Choi...

They're all Baxter Building *scientists* and *tech support.*

STORM, FRANKLIN

BAXTER BUILDING
BEARER ONLY

Johnny-- it's *Dad.*

But why would he leave his *I.D. card* on the roof? I do[n't] get...

You don't *get* it? Wow, then let's call in Sherlock *Holmes!*

If *you* don't get it, it must be pretty much *ungettable.*

What?

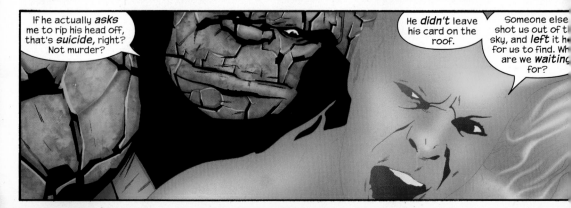

If he actually *asks* me to rip his head off, that's *suicide*, right? Not murder?

He *didn't* leave his card on the roof.

Someone else shot us out of t[he] sky, and *left* it h[ere] for us to find. Wh[y] are we *waiting* for?

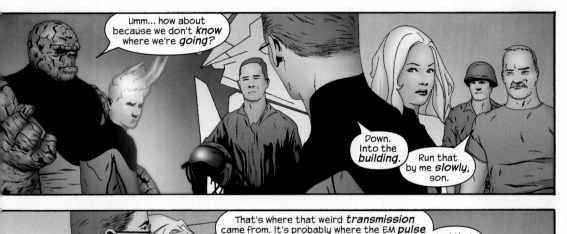

Umm... how about because we don't *know* where we're *going*?

Down. Into the *building*.

Run that by me *slowly*, son.

That's where that weird *transmission* came from. It's probably where the EM *pulse* came from, too, if it was *my* rig that was being used.

And that *door* over there--

--it was *closed* when we came down.

Now it's *open*.

I can't let you go *in* there, Richards. Any of you. Standing orders are to keep you *safe*, and this looks like a *trap*.

*Does* it? With a *trap*, the point is you're not *supposed* to see it coming.

The trapper doesn't--you know-- doesn't hang out a *sign* saying: "Caution, trap ahead."

No.

I think this is more like-- some kind of a *challenge*.

Then we don't *take* it. Half of *New York* saw us come down.

We sit tight and wait for *support* to arrive.

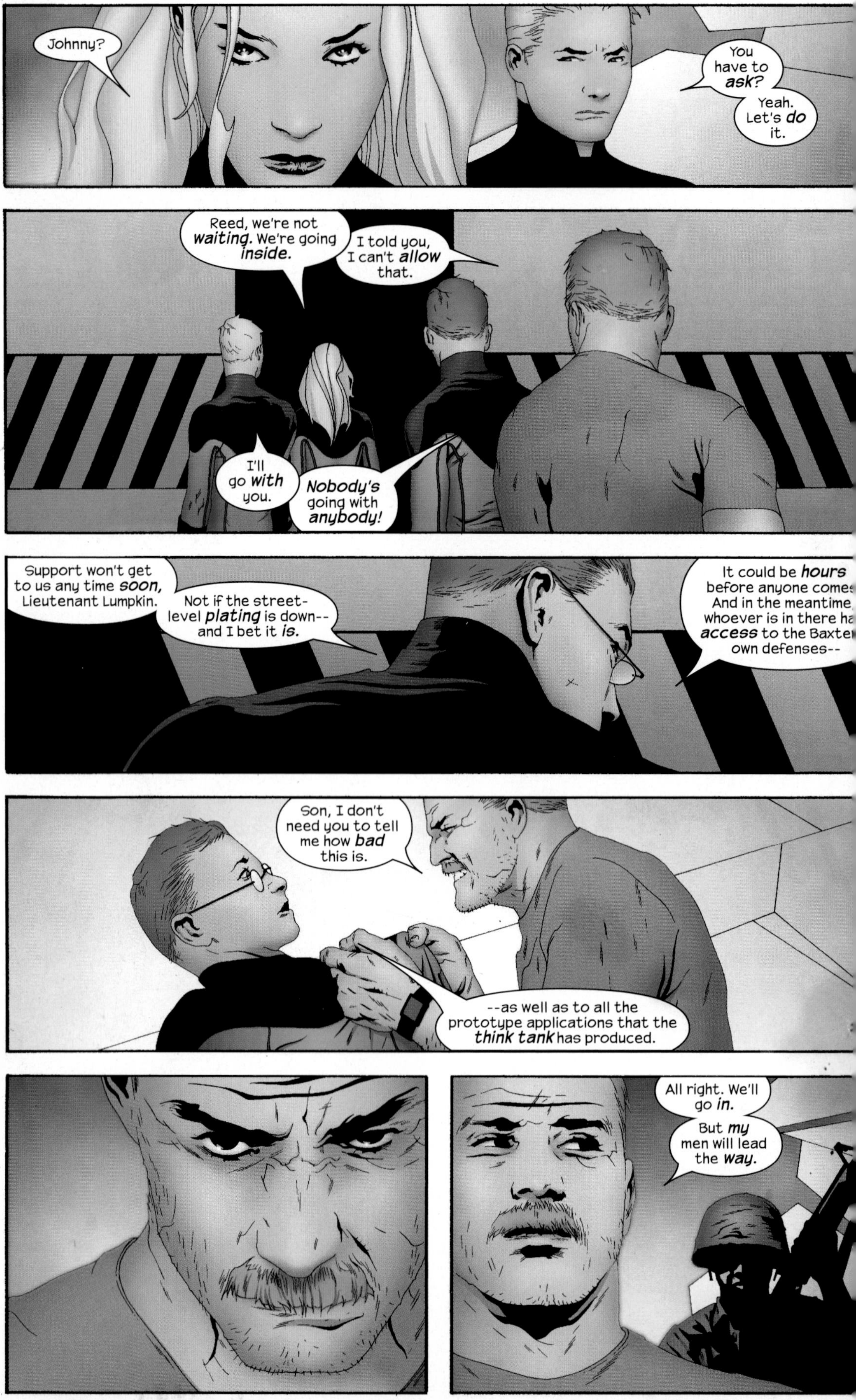

Johnny?
You have to ask?
Yeah. Let's do it.
Reed, we're not waiting. We're going inside.
I told you, I can't allow that.
I'll go with you.
Nobody's going with anybody!
Support won't get to us any time soon, Lieutenant Lumpkin.
Not if the street-level plating is down-- and I bet it is.
It could be hours before anyone come
And in the meantime
whoever is in there ha
access to the Baxte
own defenses--
Son, I don't need you to tell me how bad this is.
--as well as to all the prototype applications that the think tank has produced.
All right. We'll go in.
But my men will lead the way.

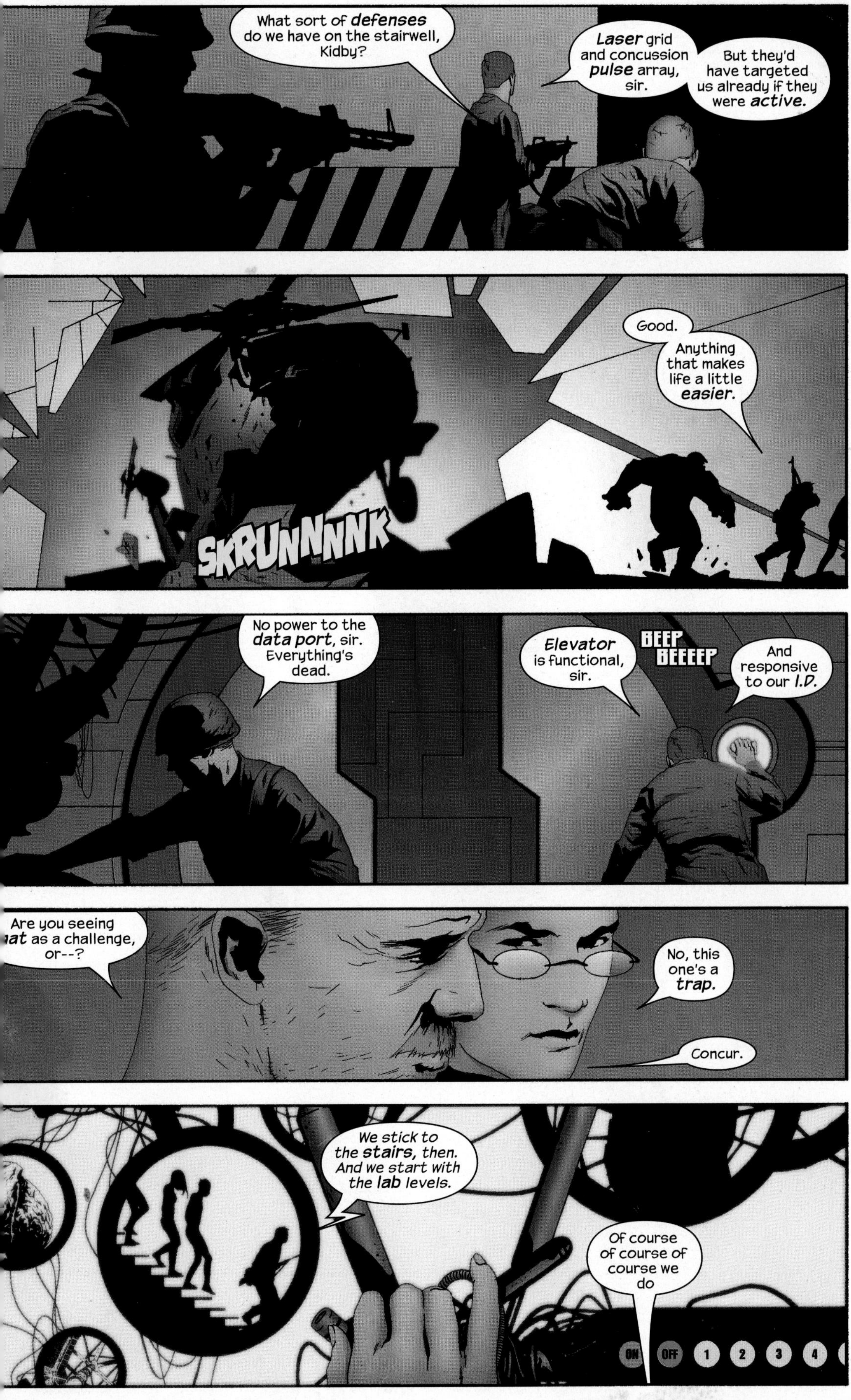
What sort of defenses do we have on the stairwell, Kidby?
Laser grid and concussion pulse array, sir.
But they'd have targeted us already if they were active.
Good.
Anything that makes life a little easier.
SKRUNNNNK
No power to the data port, sir. Everything's dead.
Elevator is functional, sir.
BEEP BEEEEP
And responsive to our I.D.
Are you seeing
at as a challenge,
or--?
No, this one's a trap.
Concur.
We stick to the stairs, then. And we start with the lab levels.
Of course of course of course we do
ON OFF 1 2 3 4

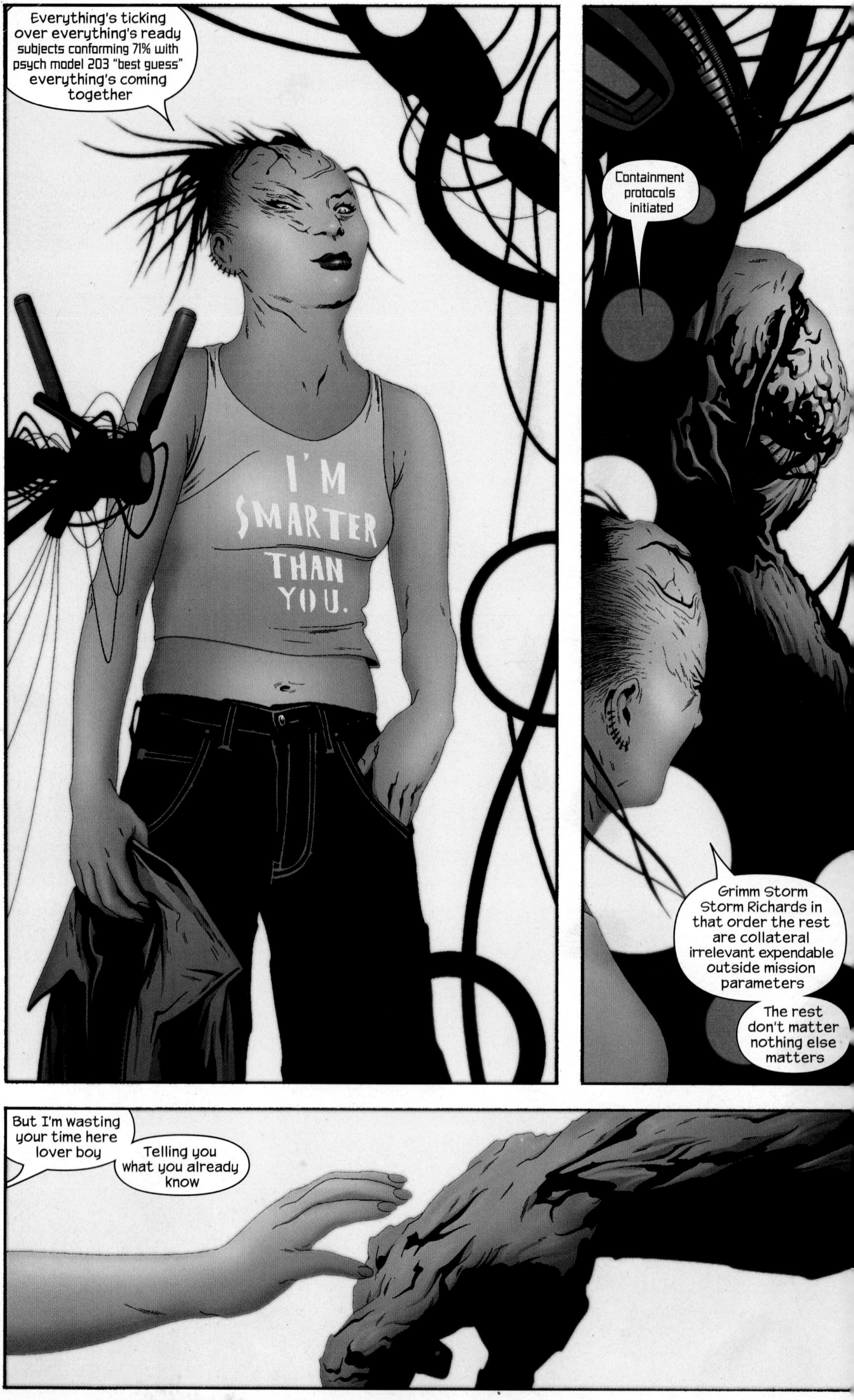

Everything's ticking over everything's ready subjects conforming 71% with psych model 203 "best guess" everything's coming together
I'M SMARTER THAN YOU.
Containment protocols initiated
Grimm Storm Storm Richards in that order the rest are collateral irrelevant expendable outside mission parameters
The rest don't matter nothing else matters
But I'm wasting your time here lover boy
Telling you what you already know

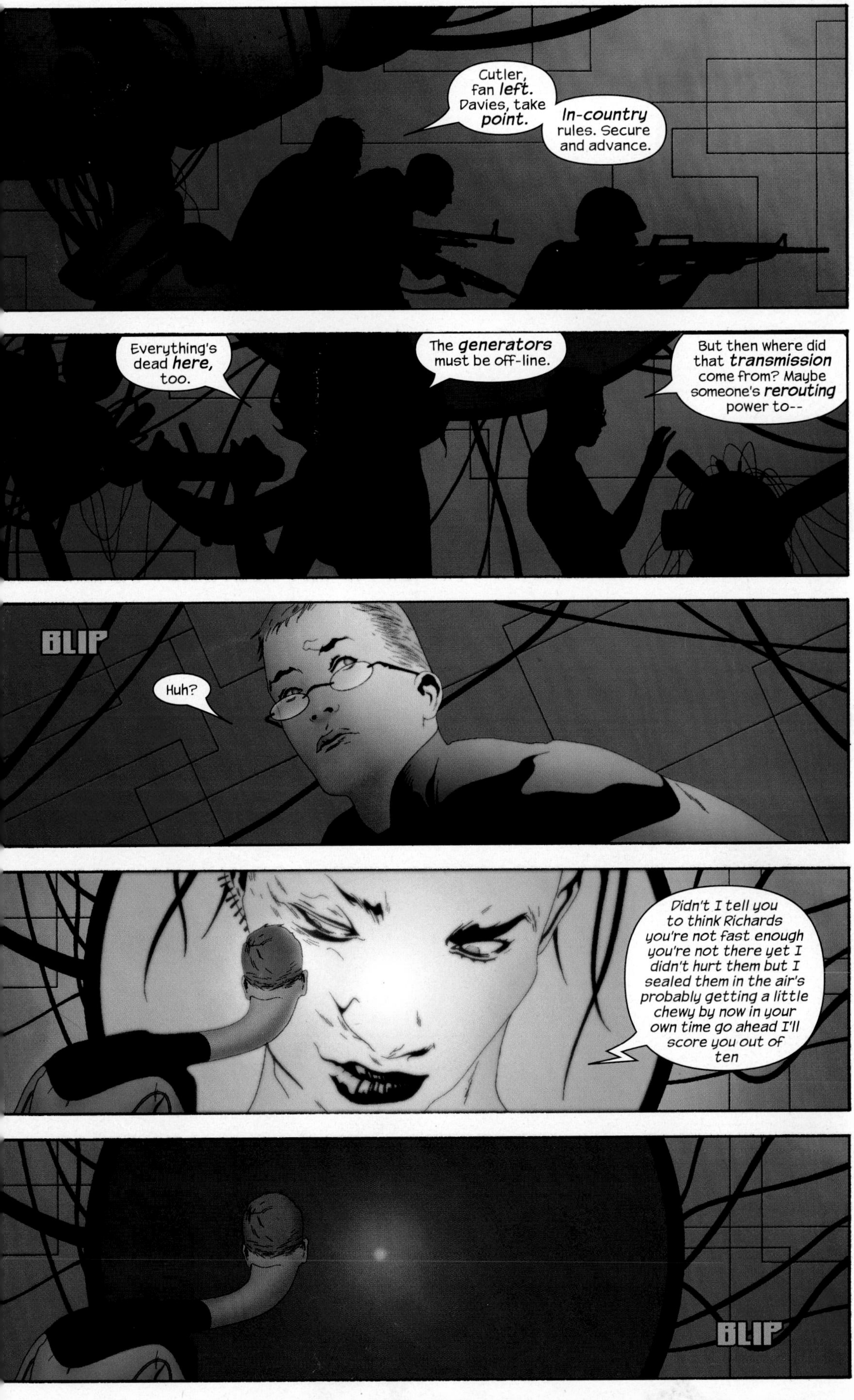

Cutler, fan left. Davies, take point.
In-country rules. Secure and advance.
Everything's dead here, too.
The generators must be off-line.
But then where did that transmission come from? Maybe someone's rerouting power to--
BLIP
Huh?
Didn't I tell you to think Richards you're not fast enough you're not there yet I didn't hurt them but I sealed them in the air's probably getting a little chewy by now in your own time go ahead I'll score you out of ten
BLIP

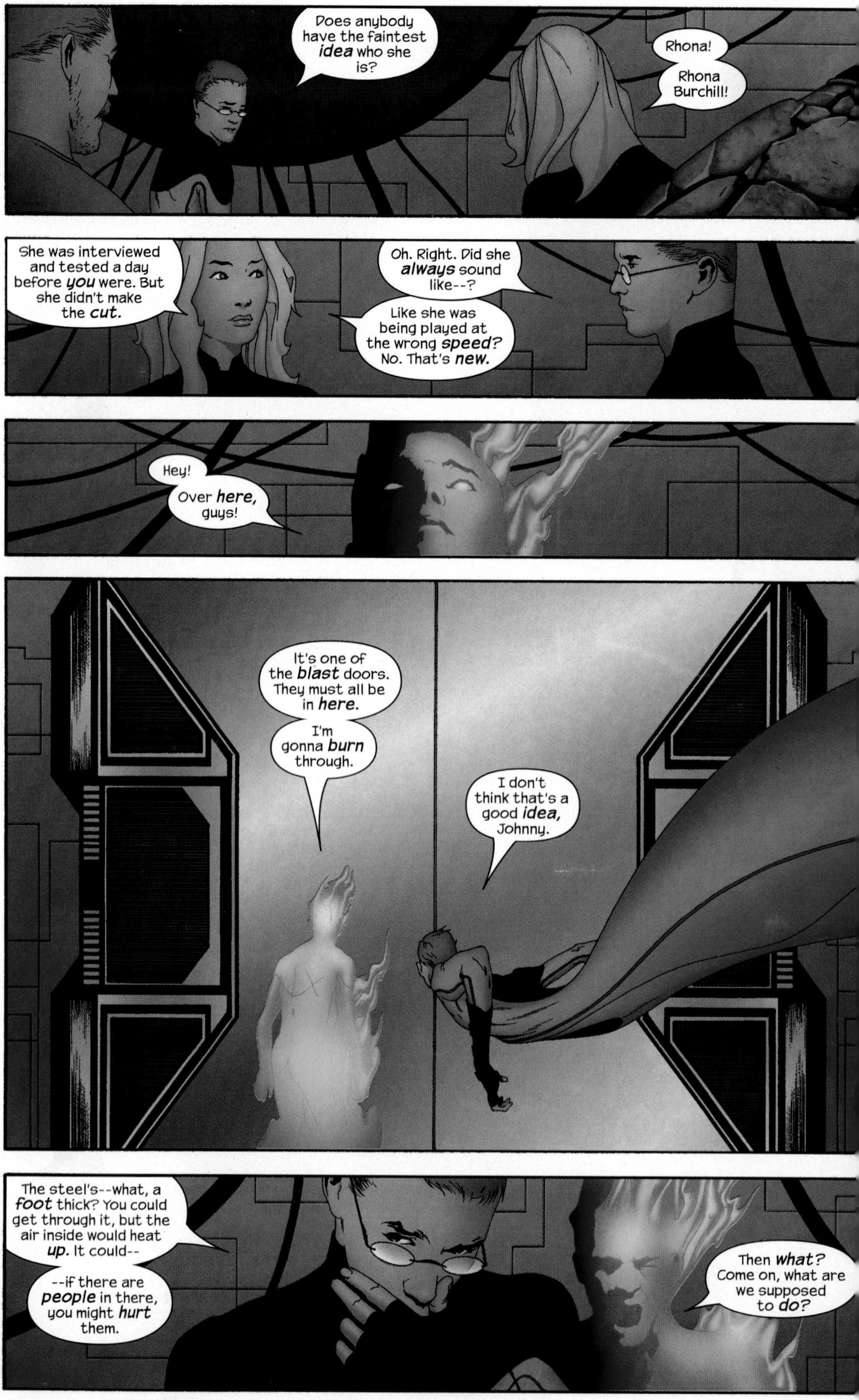

Does anybody have the faintest idea who she is?
Rhona!
Rhona Burchill!
She was interviewed and tested a day before you were. But she didn't make the cut.
Oh. Right. Did she always sound like--?
Like she was being played at the wrong speed? No. That's new.
Hey!
Over here, guys!
It's one of the blast doors. They must all be in here.
I'm gonna burn through.
I don't think that's a good idea, Johnny.
The steel's--what, a foot thick? You could get through it, but the air inside would heat up. It could--
--if there are people in there, you might hurt them.
Then what? Come on, what are we supposed to do?

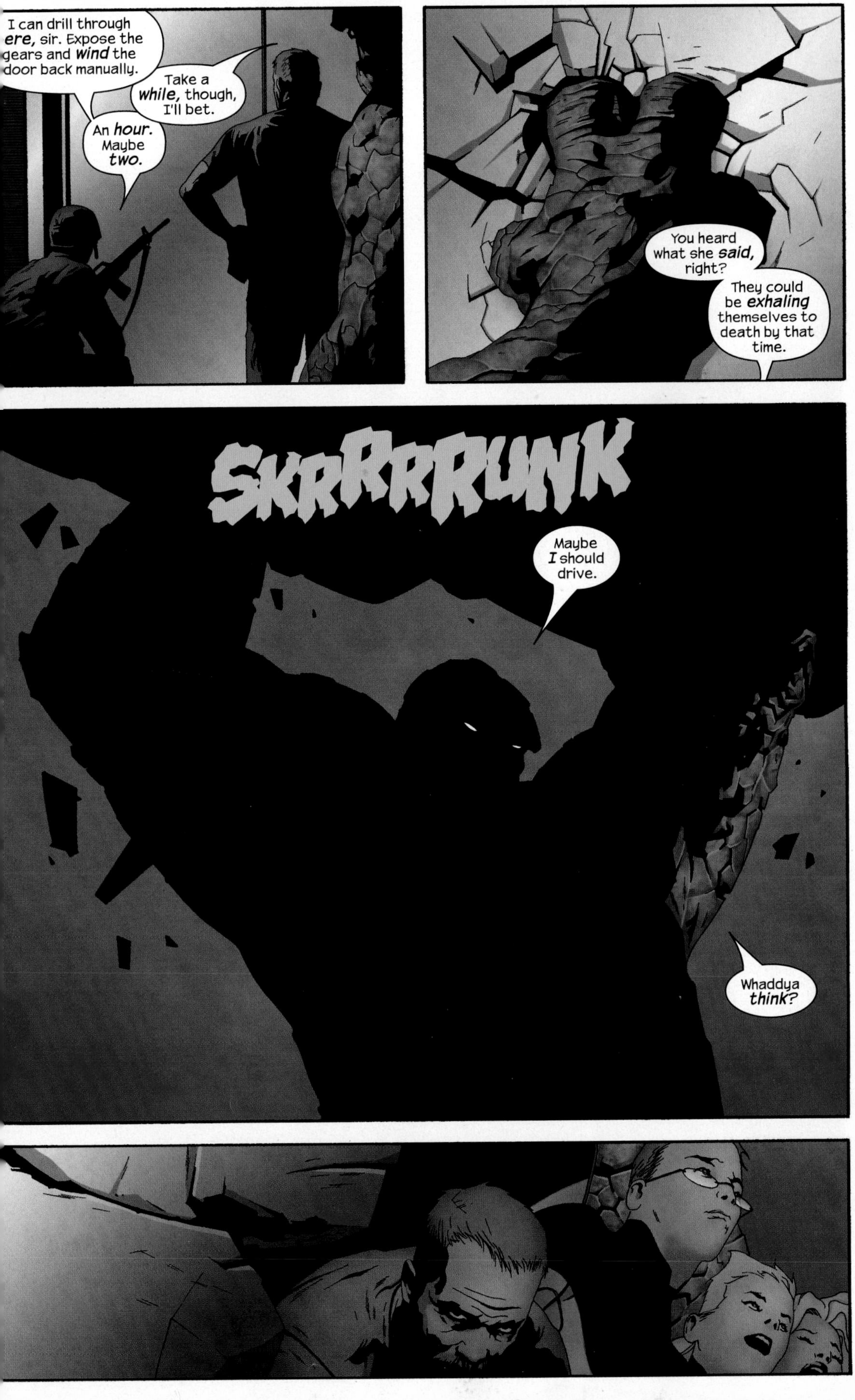

I can drill through
ere, sir. Expose the gears and wind the door back manually.
Take a while, though, I'll bet.
An hour. Maybe two.
You heard what she said, right?
They could be exhaling themselves to death by that time.
SKRRRRUNK
Maybe I should drive.
Whaddya think?

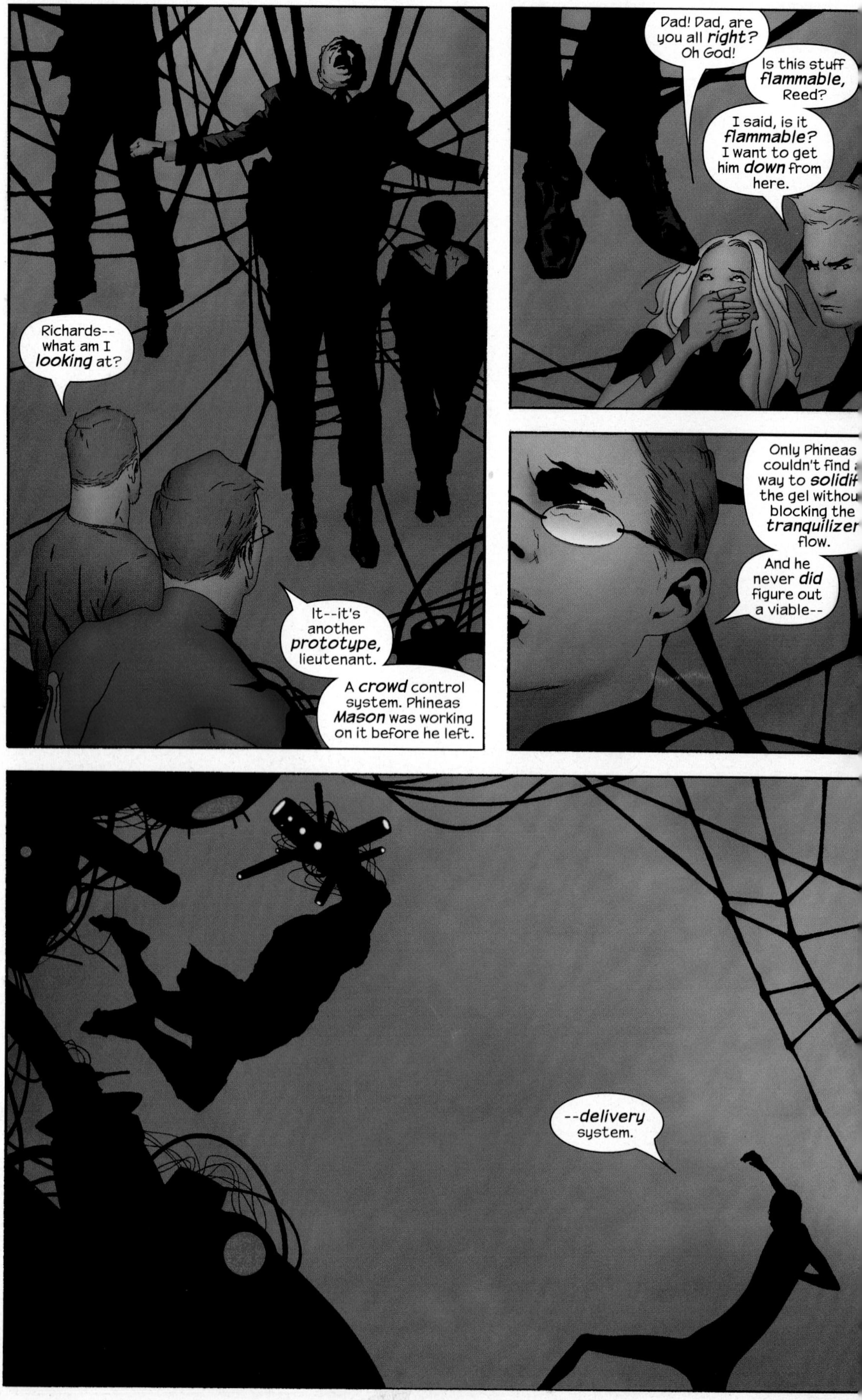
Richards-- what am I looking at?
It--it's another prototype, lieutenant.
A crowd control system. Phineas Mason was working on it before he left.
Dad! Dad, are you all right? Oh God!
Is this stuff flammable, Reed?
I said, is it flammable? I want to get him down from here.
Only Phineas couldn't find a way to solidify the gel without blocking the tranquilizer flow.
And he never did figure out a viable--
--delivery system.

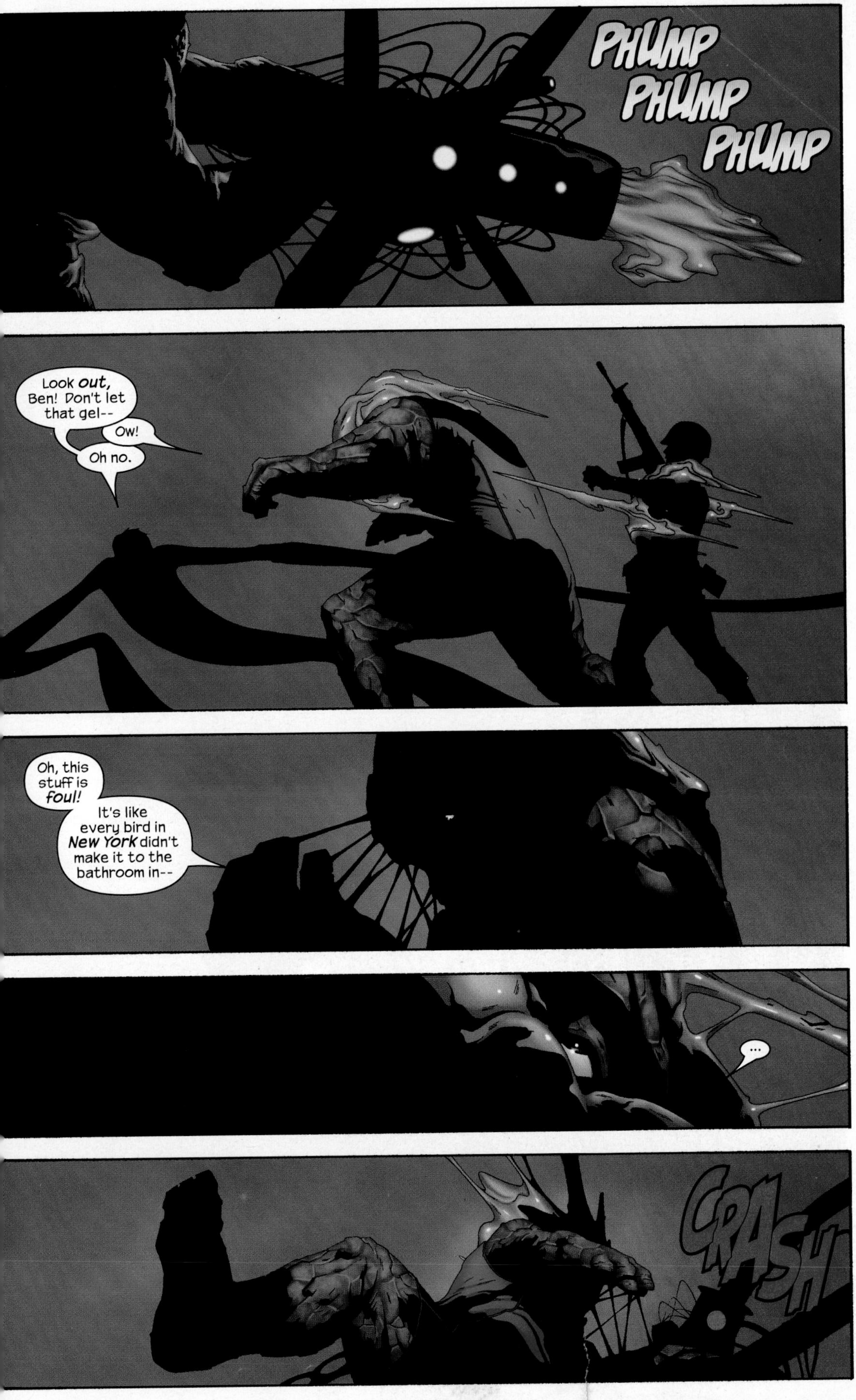
PHUMP
PHUMP
PHUMP
Look out, Ben! Don't let that gel--
Ow!
Oh no.
Oh, this stuff is foul!
It's like every bird in New York didn't make it to the bathroom in--
...
CRASH

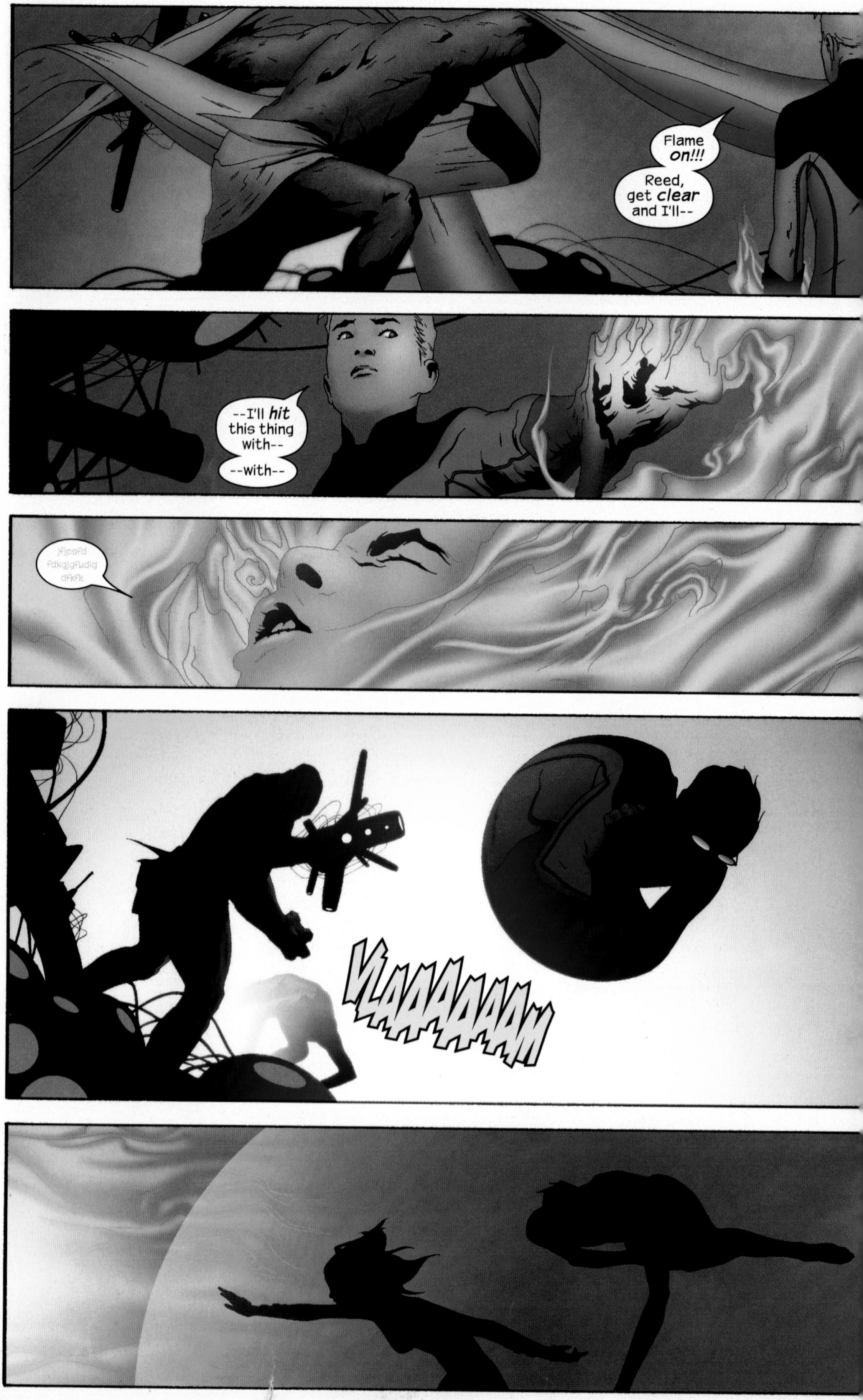
Flame *on!!!*
Reed, get *clear* and I'll--
--I'll *hit* this thing with--
--with--
jfjpsfd fdkgjgfudig dfkfk
VLAAAAAAM

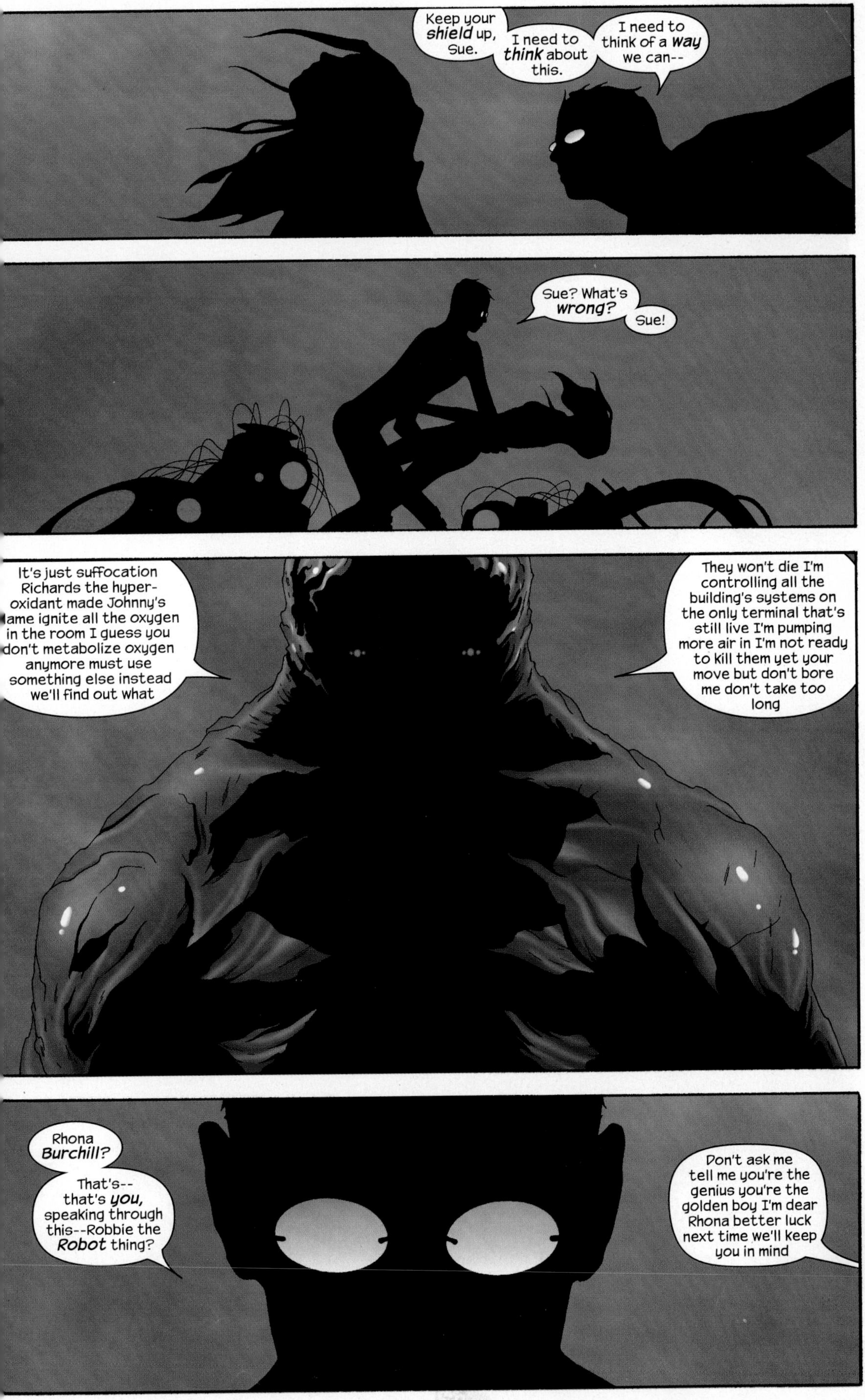
Keep your shield up, Sue.
I need to think about this.
I need to think of a way we can--
Sue? What's wrong?
Sue!
It's just suffocation Richards the hyper-oxidant made Johnny's ame ignite all the oxygen in the room I guess you don't metabolize oxygen anymore must use something else instead we'll find out what
They won't die I'm controlling all the building's systems on the only terminal that's still live I'm pumping more air in I'm not ready to kill them yet your move but don't bore me don't take too long
Rhona Burchill?
That's-- that's you, speaking through this--Robbie the Robot thing?
Don't ask me tell me you're the genius you're the golden boy I'm dear Rhona better luck next time we'll keep you in mind

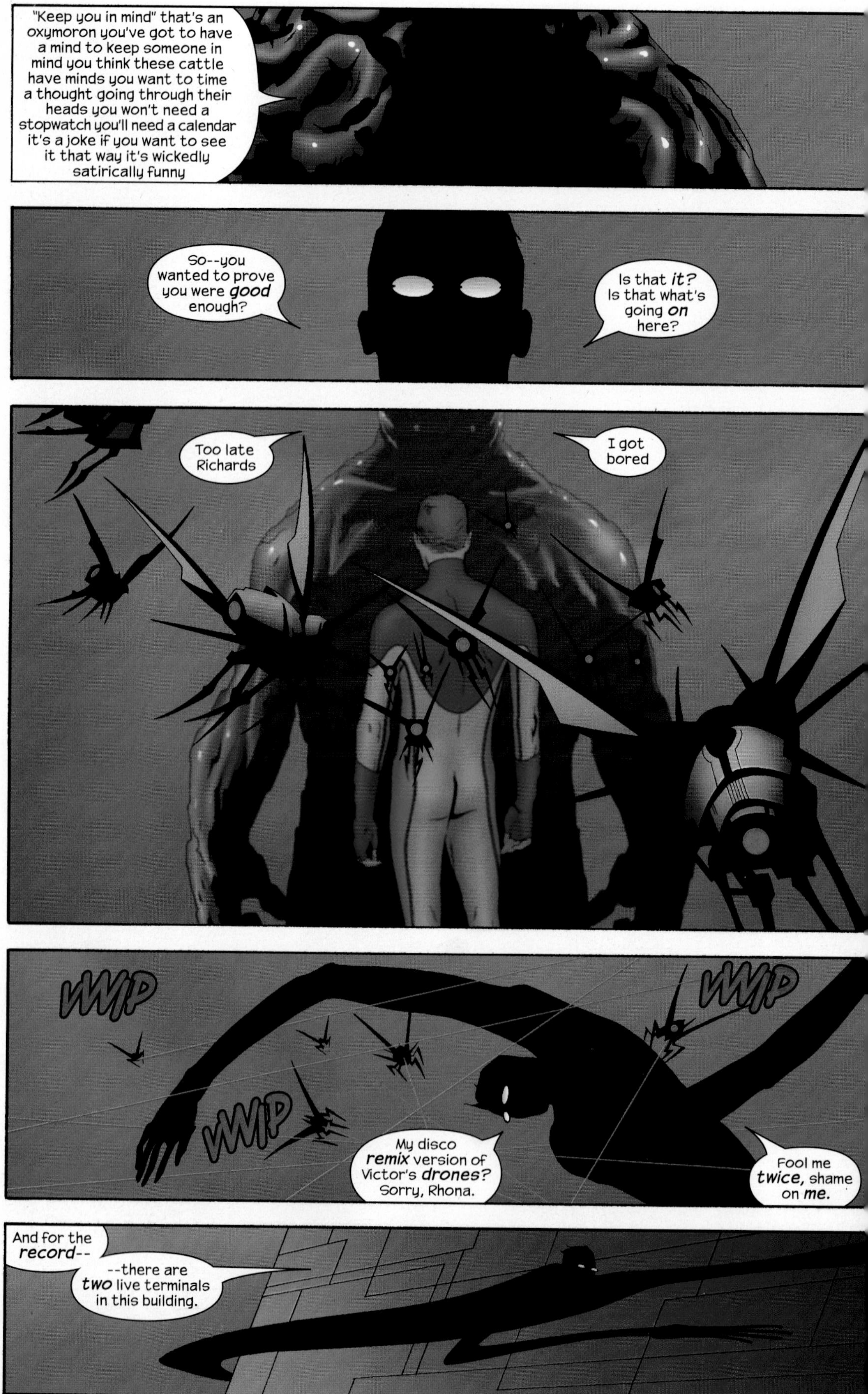
"Keep you in mind" that's an oxymoron you've got to have a mind to keep someone in mind you think these cattle have minds you want to time a thought going through their heads you won't need a stopwatch you'll need a calendar it's a joke if you want to see it that way it's wickedly satirically funny
So--you wanted to prove you were good enough?
Is that it? Is that what's going on here?
Too late Richards
I got bored
VWIP
VWIP
VWIP
My disco remix version of Victor's drones? Sorry, Rhona.
Fool me twice, shame on me.
And for the record--
--there are two live terminals in this building.

You left one up and *running* so you could stick your *tongue* out at us.
Remember?
TEK TEK TEK
BUILDING SECURITY ACCESS PASSWORD REQUIRED
******
RETYPE PASSWORD
******
SYSTEM FOLDER
CONTROL GLOBAL SHUT-OUT
PARAMETERS REMOTE
PARAMETERS AUTOMATIC
PARAMETERS MOVEMENT-ACTIVATED
PARAMETERS HEAT-ACTIVATED
PARAMETERS DEFAULT
DEFAULT RETURN TO TERMINAL
TERMINAL IDENT 12294765868
RETYPE TERMINAL IDENT
BLIP
YES
OF
COURSE
I
REMEMBER
FWAAAASHHHH

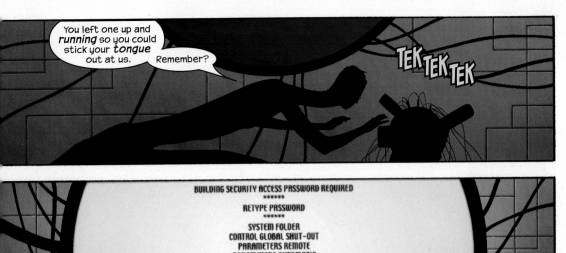

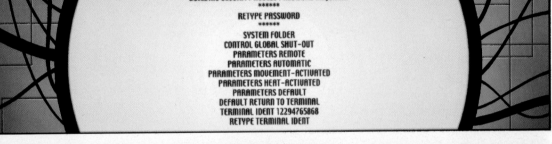

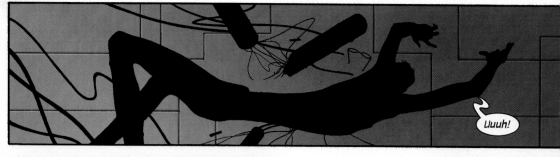

Uuuh!

You see Richards you don't need a think tank you just need a thinker one thinker will do it if she's using all she's got that's me you arrogant little snot you waste of synapses that's me

You're going to hate the next part really really

really ha

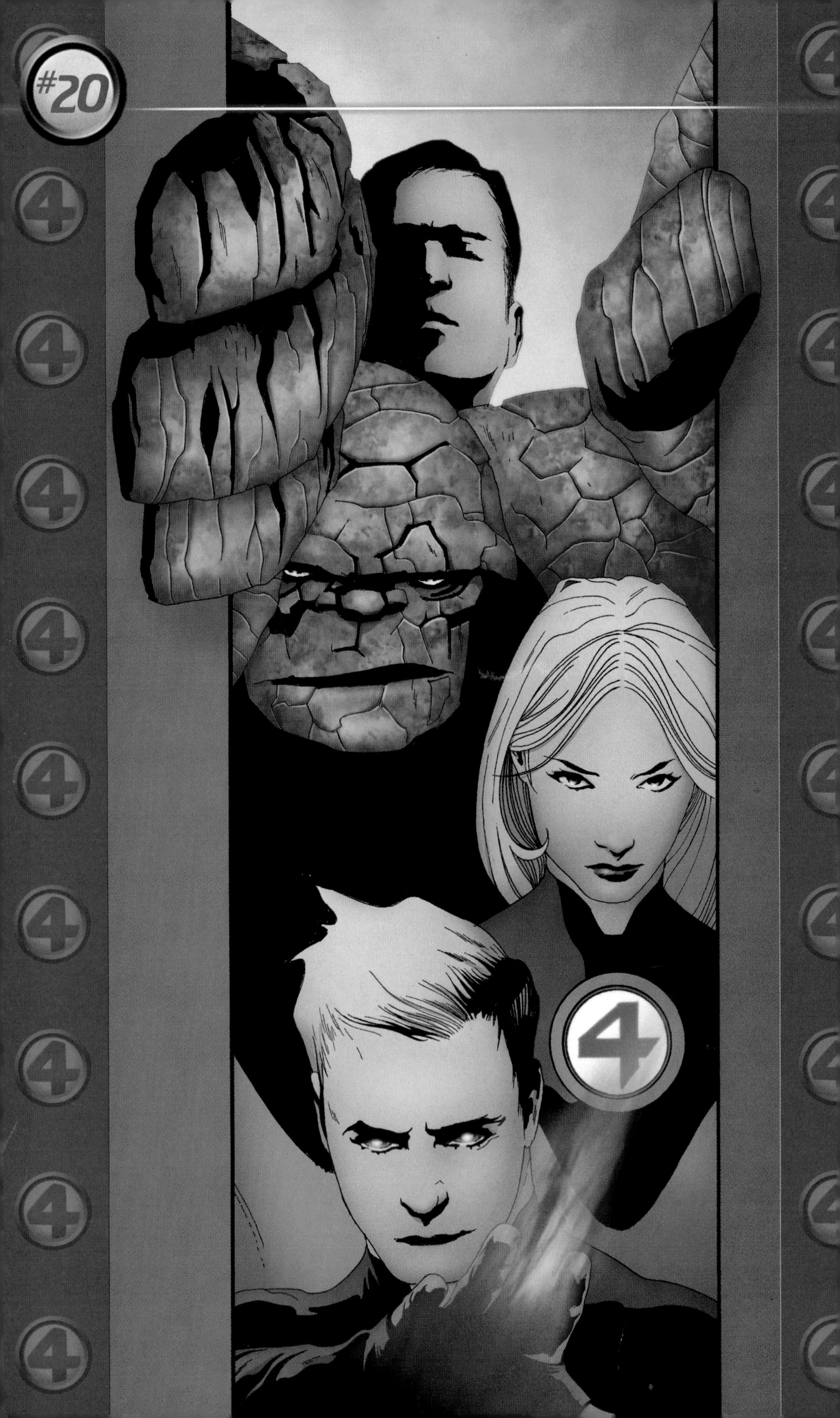
#20

# THINK TANK

PART 2 OF 2

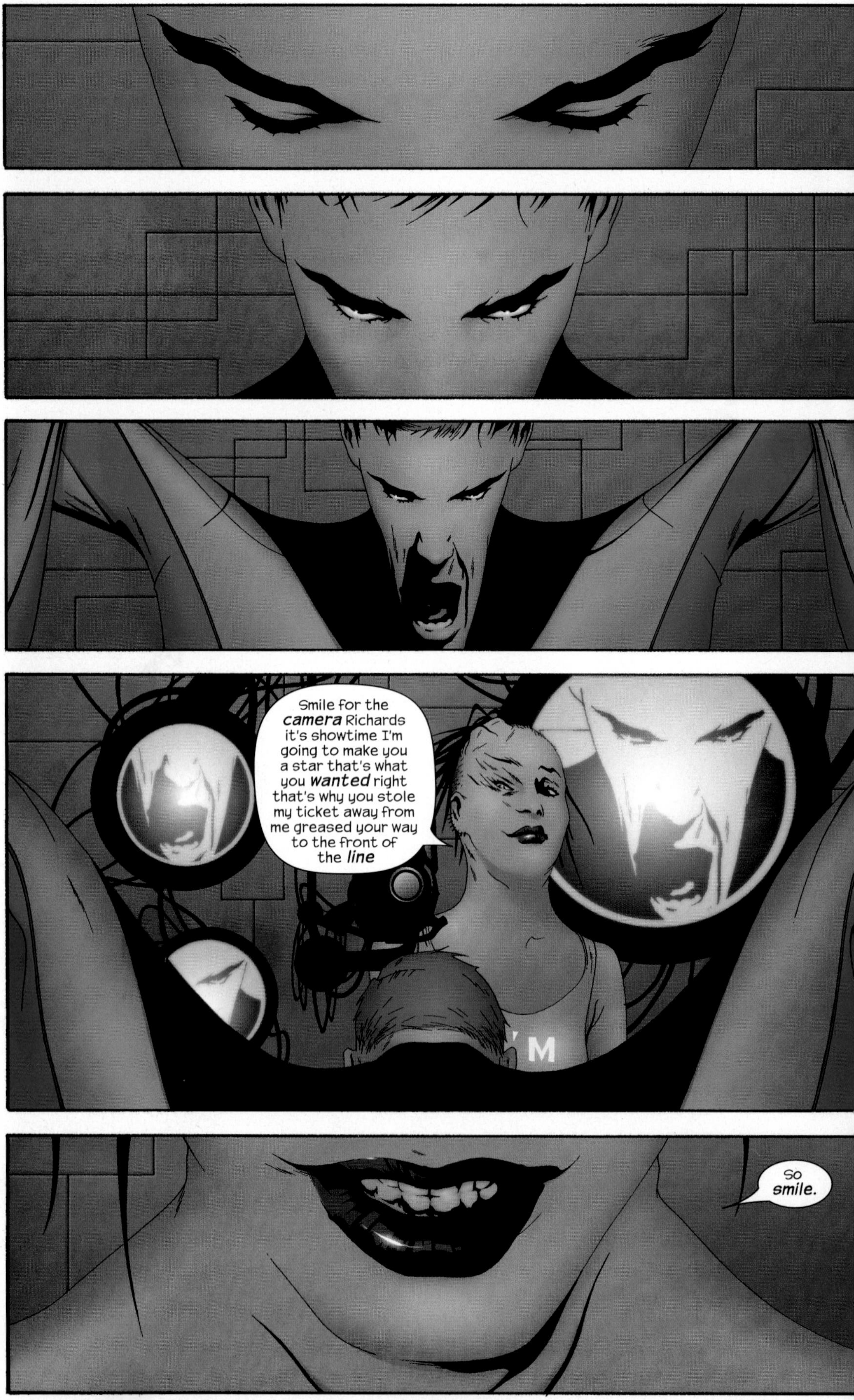
Smile for the camera Richards it's showtime I'm going to make you a star that's what you wanted right that's why you stole my ticket away from me greased your way to the front of the line
So smile.

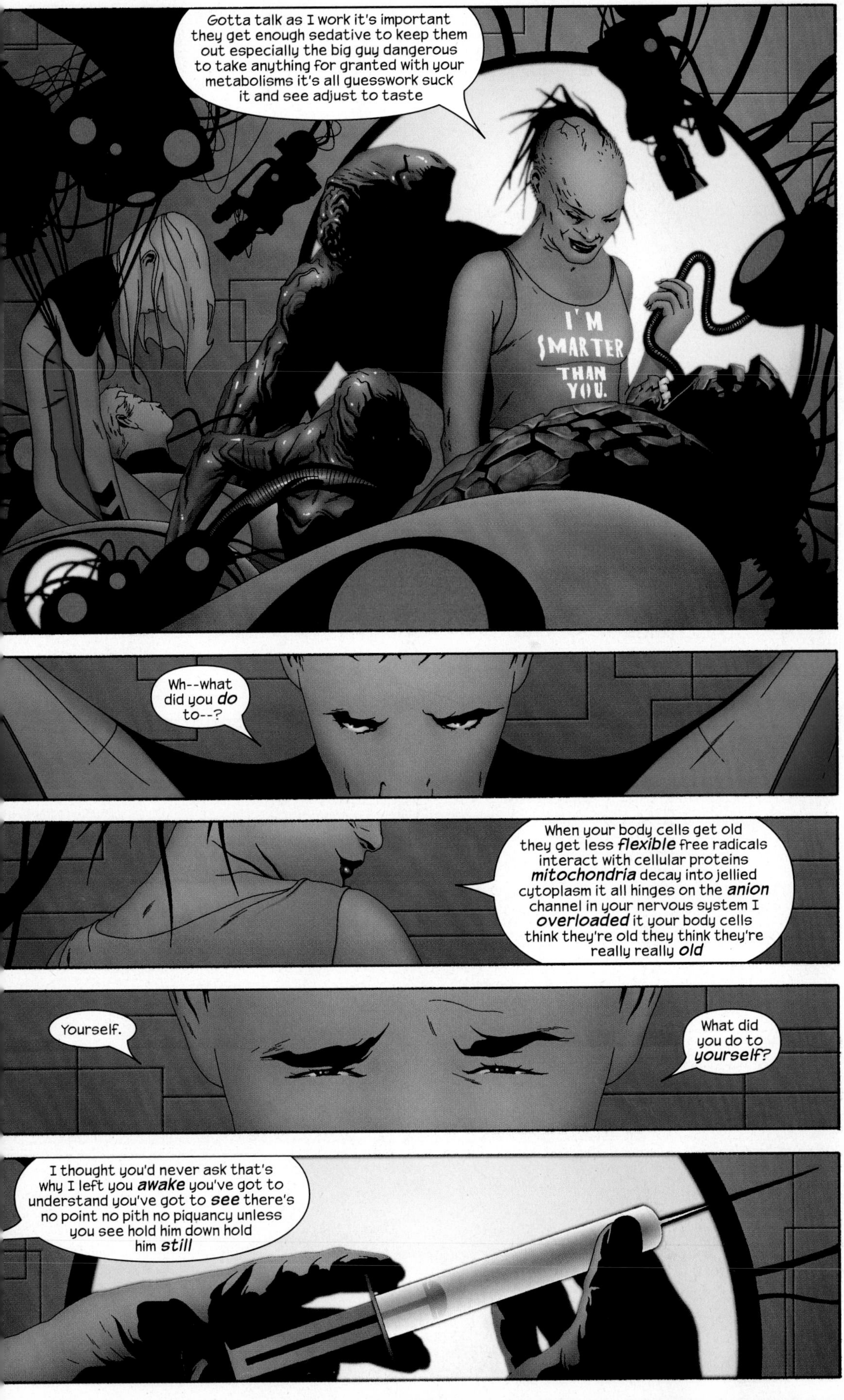
Gotta talk as I work it's important they get enough sedative to keep them out especially the big guy dangerous to take anything for granted with your metabolisms it's all guesswork suck it and see adjust to taste
I'M SMARTER THAN YOU.
Wh--what did you do to--?
When your body cells get old they get less flexible free radicals interact with cellular proteins mitochondria decay into jellied cytoplasm it all hinges on the anion channel in your nervous system I overloaded it your body cells think they're old they think they're really really old
Yourself.
What did you do to yourself?
I thought you'd never ask that's why I left you awake you've got to understand you've got to see there's no point no pith no piquancy unless you see hold him down hold him still

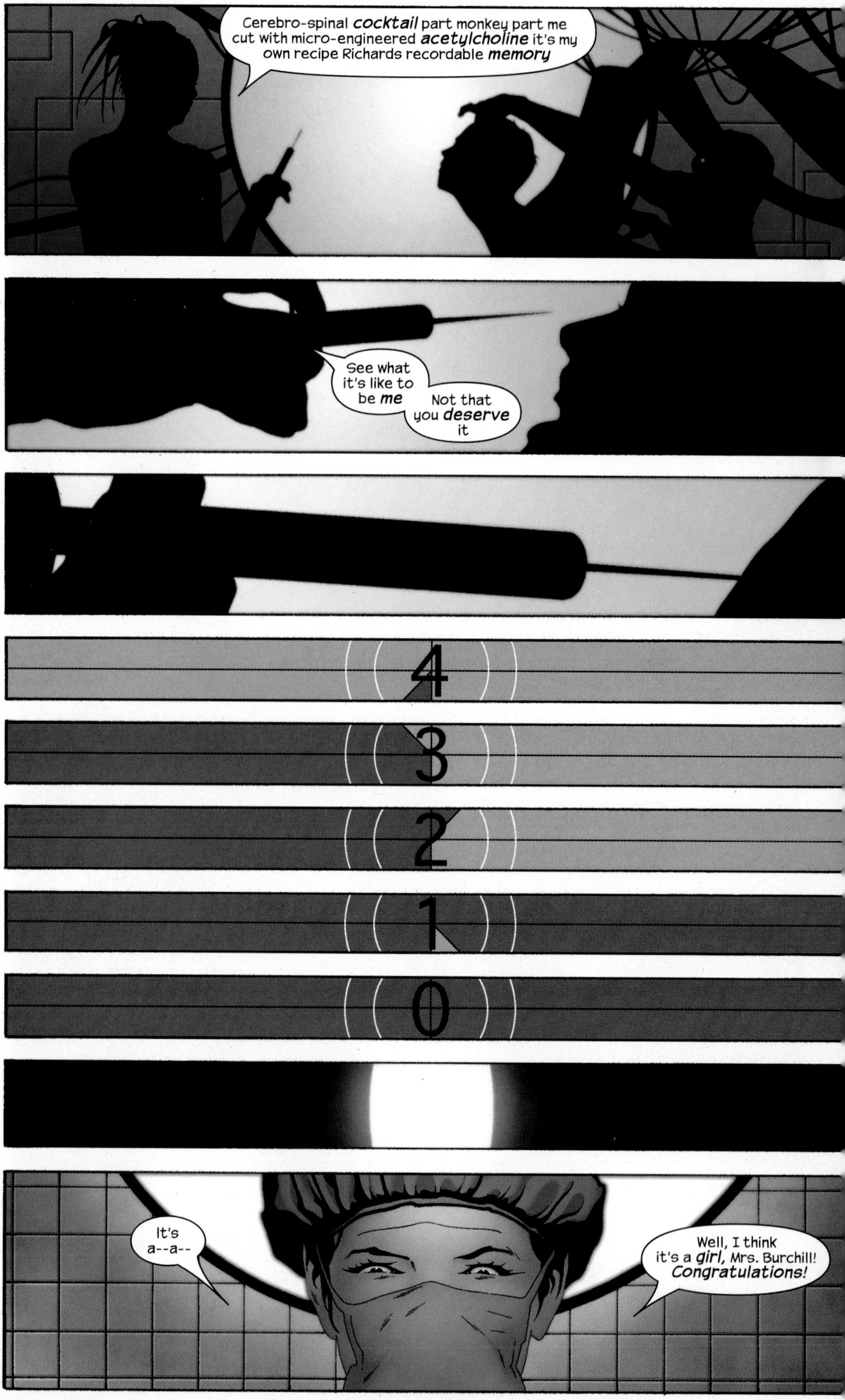
Cerebro-spinal cocktail part monkey part me cut with micro-engineered acetylcholine it's my own recipe Richards recordable memory
See what it's like to be me
Not that you deserve it
4
3
2
1
0
It's a--a--
Well, I think it's a girl, Mrs. Burchill! Congratulations!

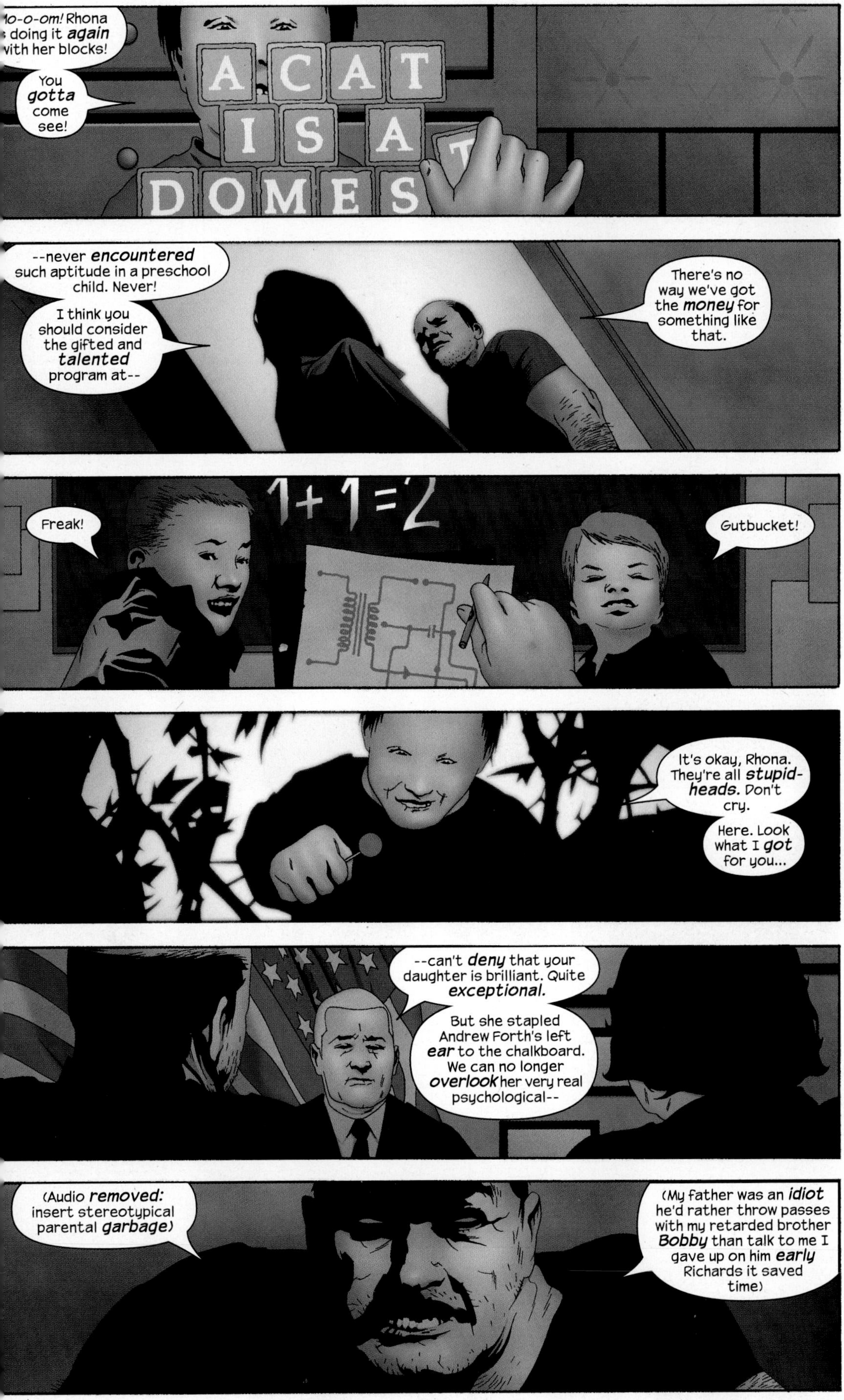

lo-o-om! Rhona
s doing it again
with her blocks!
You gotta come see!
A CAT IS A T DOMES
--never encountered such aptitude in a preschool child. Never!
I think you should consider the gifted and talented program at--
There's no way we've got the money for something like that.
1+1=2
Freak!
Gutbucket!
It's okay, Rhona. They're all stupid-heads. Don't cry.
Here. Look what I got for you...
--can't deny that your daughter is brilliant. Quite exceptional.
But she stapled Andrew Forth's left ear to the chalkboard. We can no longer overlook her very real psychological--
(Audio removed: insert stereotypical parental garbage)
(My father was an idiot he'd rather throw passes with my retarded brother Bobby than talk to me I gave up on him early Richards it saved time)

(late-night mommy-daddy *conference*, supposedly after I've gone to *sleep*)

(summary: we can't *afford* to send her to a private school, so what are we going to *do?*)

(boo-hoo, sob sob)

BONG
CLANG

Mr. Burchill? My name is *Lumpkin*.

I know it's *late*, but I wonder if we could *talk?*

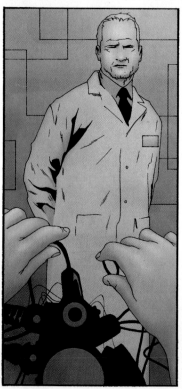

So she's not *good* enough?

Mr. Burchill, your daughter's *intellect* is staggering. But so is her *psych* profile.

You ain't gonna *take* 'er?

We can't *support* her.

*Knew* it was too good to be true. Tellin' us you were something *special.*

Reed *Richards?* Welcome to the Baxter Building!

Well, young man, I have some good *news* for you.

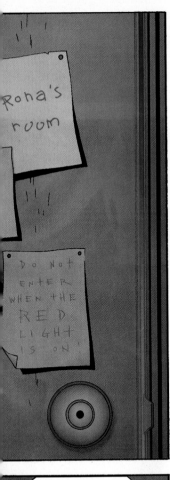

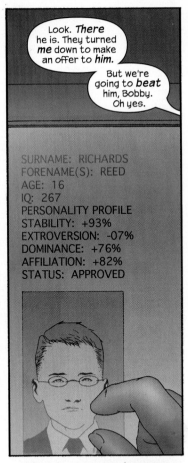

Rona's room
Do not enter when the RED light is on!
Look. There he is. They turned me down to make an offer to him.
But we're going to beat him, Bobby. Oh yes.
SURNAME: RICHARDS
FORENAME(S): REED
AGE: 16
IQ: 267
PERSONALITY PROFILE
STABILITY: +93%
EXTROVERSION: -07%
DOMINANCE: +76%
AFFILIATION: +82%
STATUS: APPROVED
Is this--is this gonna hurt, Rhona?
Of course it won't hurt. That's what the anesthetic is for.
See, it's easy to increase my processing speed. I just remove the latency period between neuron firings. Bingo. Six hundred percent efficiency.
But I need extra capacity, Bobby. I need more brain mass. Compatible brain mass.
And it's not like you were using it.
Now we'll see Richards now we'll see what we'll see what we'll see what we'll

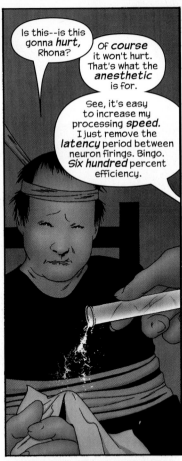

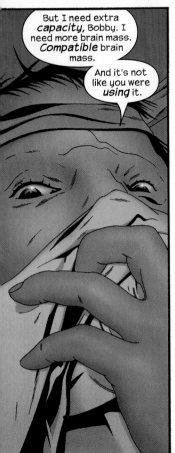

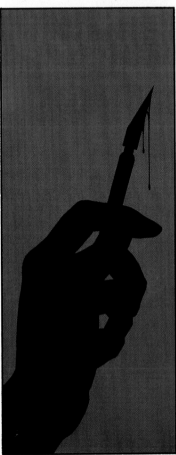

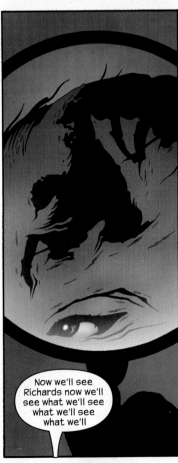

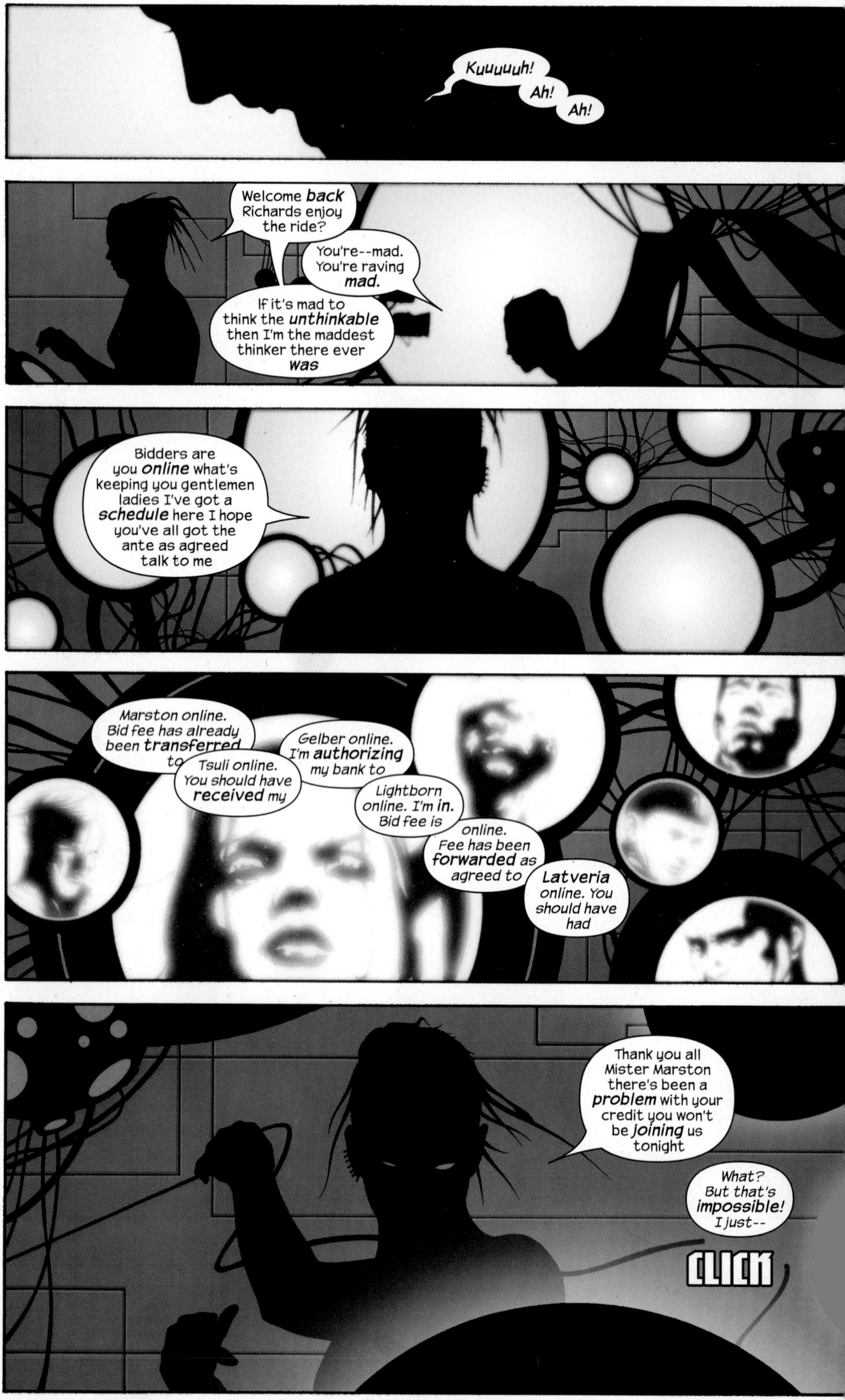

Kuuuuuh! Ah! Ah!
Welcome back Richards enjoy the ride?
You're--mad. You're raving mad.
If it's mad to think the unthinkable then I'm the maddest thinker there ever was
Bidders are you online what's keeping you gentlemen ladies I've got a schedule here I hope you've all got the ante as agreed talk to me
Marston online. Bid fee has already been transferred to
Gelber online. I'm authorizing my bank to
Tsuli online. You should have received my
Lightborn online. I'm in. Bid fee is
online. Fee has been forwarded as agreed to
Latveria online. You should have had
Thank you all Mister Marston there's been a problem with your credit you won't be joining us tonight
What? But that's impossible! I just--
CLICK

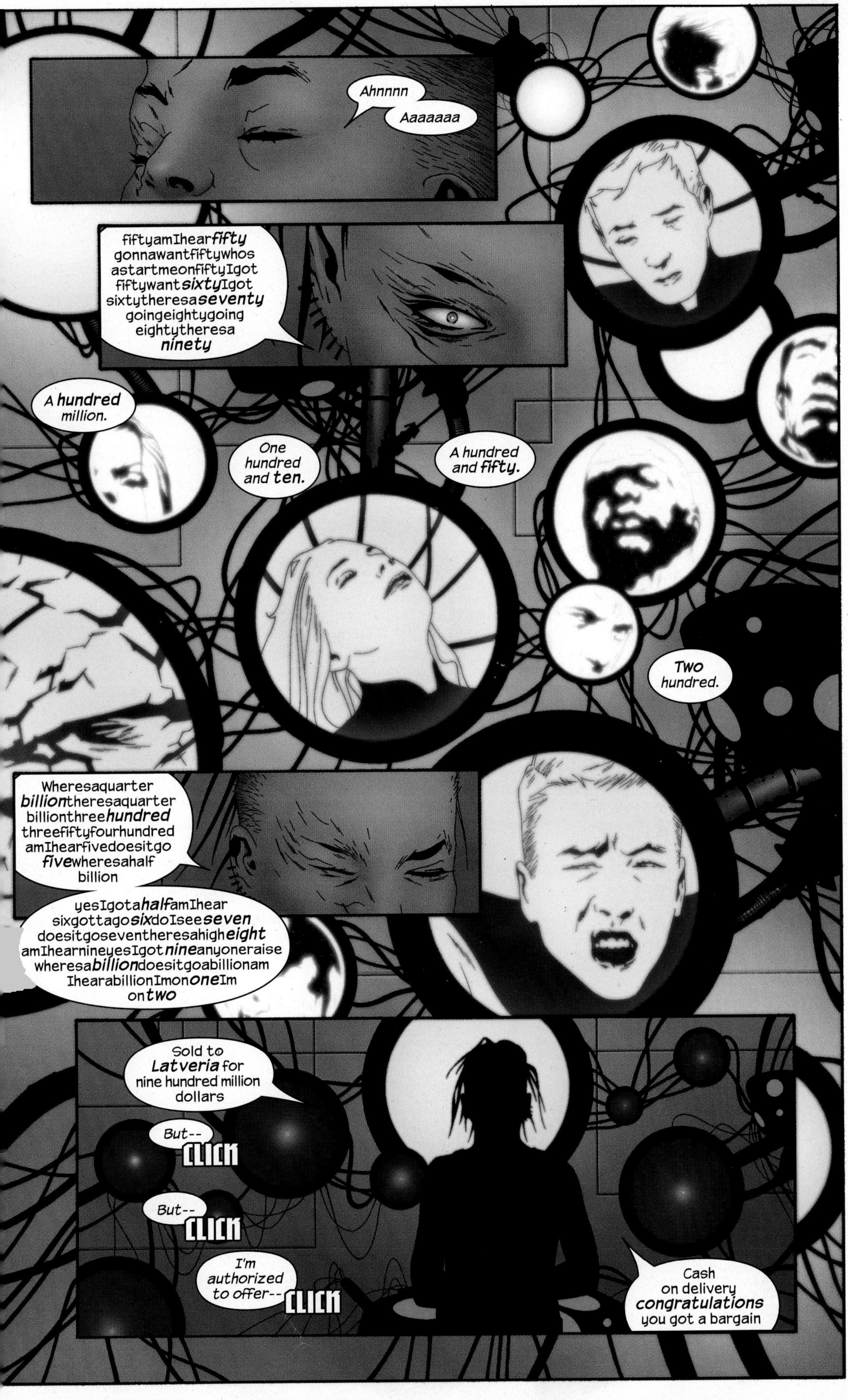
Ahnnnn
Aaaaaaa
fiftyamIhearfifty gonnawantfiftywhos astartmeonfiftyIgot fiftywantsixtyIgot sixtytheresaseventy goingeightygoing eightytheresa ninety
A hundred million.
One hundred and ten.
A hundred and fifty.
Two hundred.
Wheresaquarter billiontheresaquarter billionthreehundred threefiftyfourhundred amIhearfivedoesitgo fivewheresahalf billion
yesIgotahalfamIhear sixgottagosixdoIseeseven doesitgoseventheresahigheight amIhearnineyesIgotnineanyoneraise wheresabilliondoesitgoabillionam IhearabillionImononeIm ontwo
Sold to Latveria for nine hundred million dollars
But--
CLICK
But--
CLICK
I'm authorized to offer--
CLICK
Cash on delivery congratulations you got a bargain

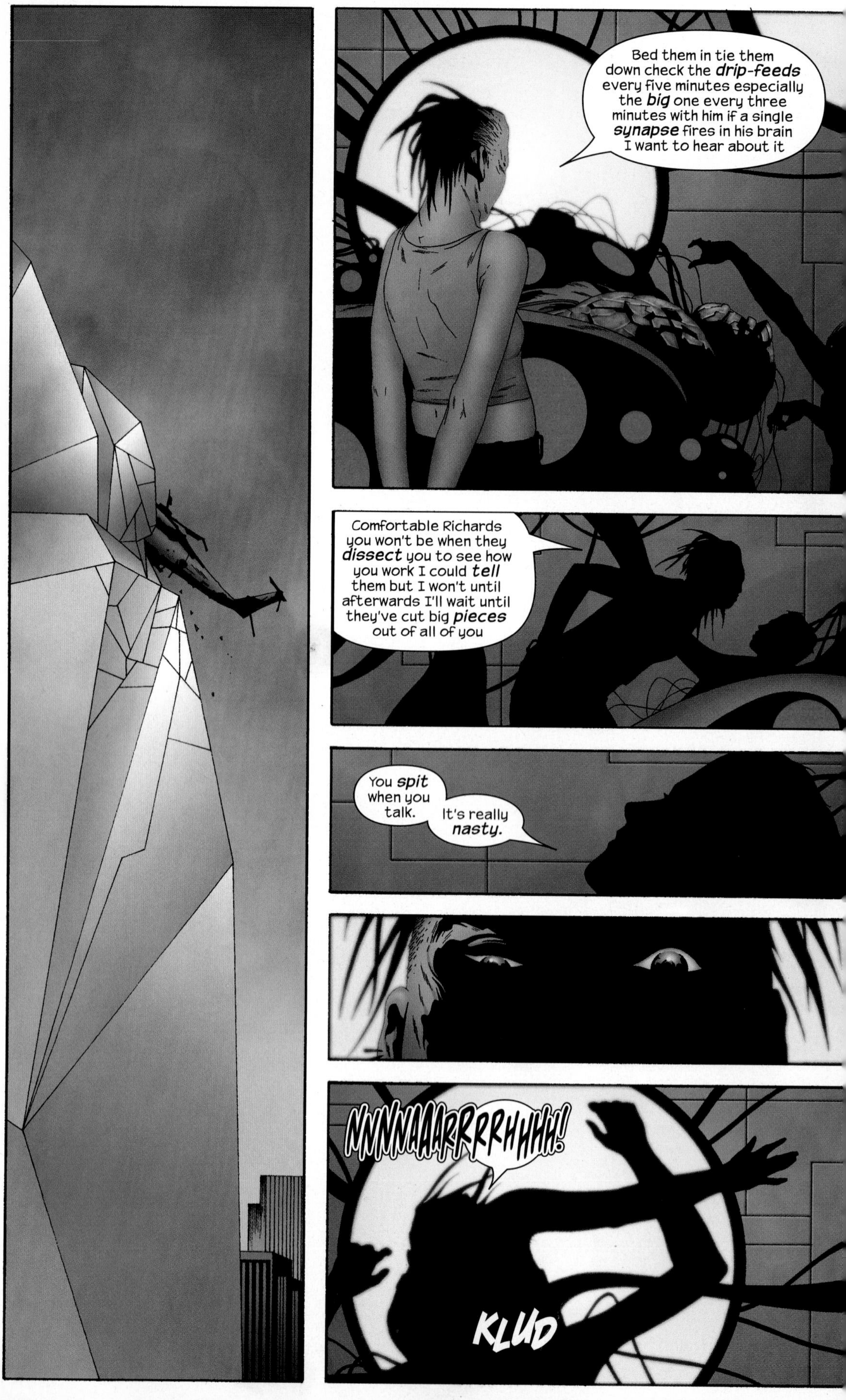
Bed them in tie them down check the *drip-feeds* every five minutes especially the *big* one every three minutes with him if a single *synapse* fires in his brain I want to hear about it
Comfortable Richards you won't be when they *dissect* you to see how you work I could *tell* them but I won't until afterwards I'll wait until they've cut big *pieces* out of all of you
You *spit* when you talk.
It's really *nasty.*
NNNNAAARRRRHHHH!
KLUD

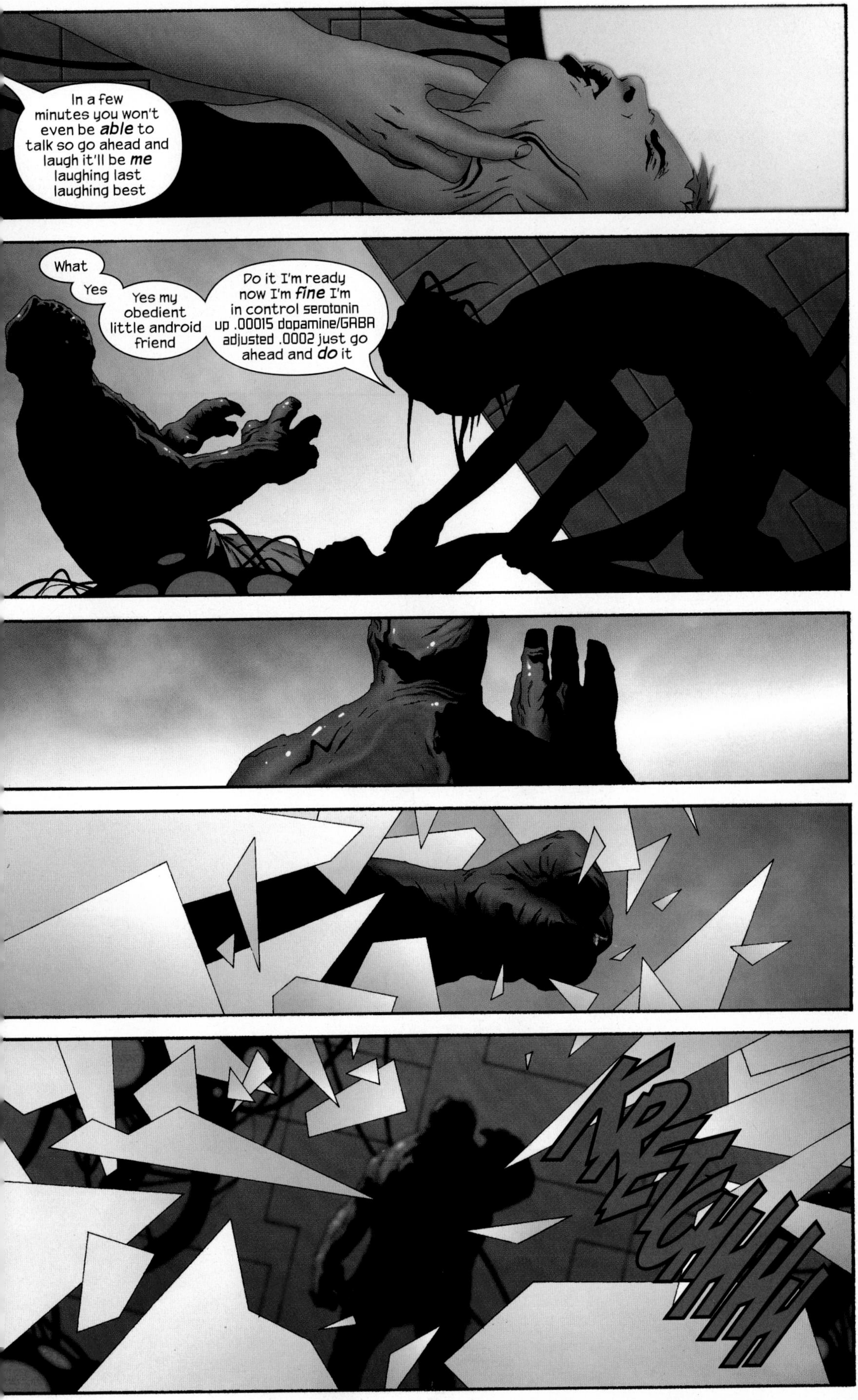
In a few minutes you won't even be *able* to talk so go ahead and laugh it'll be *me* laughing last laughing best
What
Yes
Yes my obedient little android friend
Do it I'm ready now I'm *fine* I'm in control serotonin up .00015 dopamine/GABA adjusted .0002 just go ahead and *do* it
KRETCHHHH

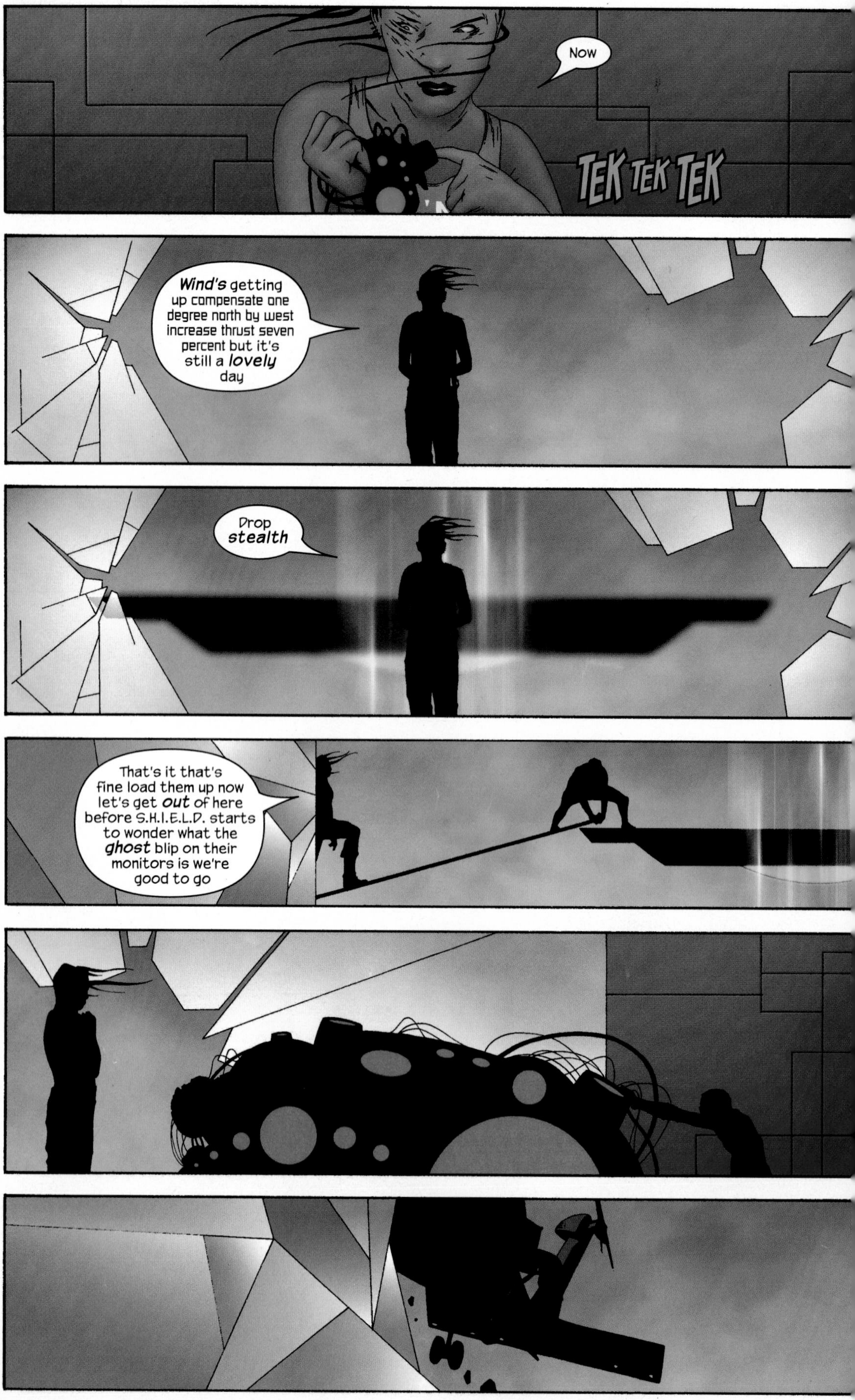
Now
TEK TEK TEK
Wind's getting up compensate one degree north by west increase thrust seven percent but it's still a lovely day
Drop stealth
That's it that's fine load them up now let's get out of here before S.H.I.E.L.D. starts to wonder what the ghost blip on their monitors is we're good to go

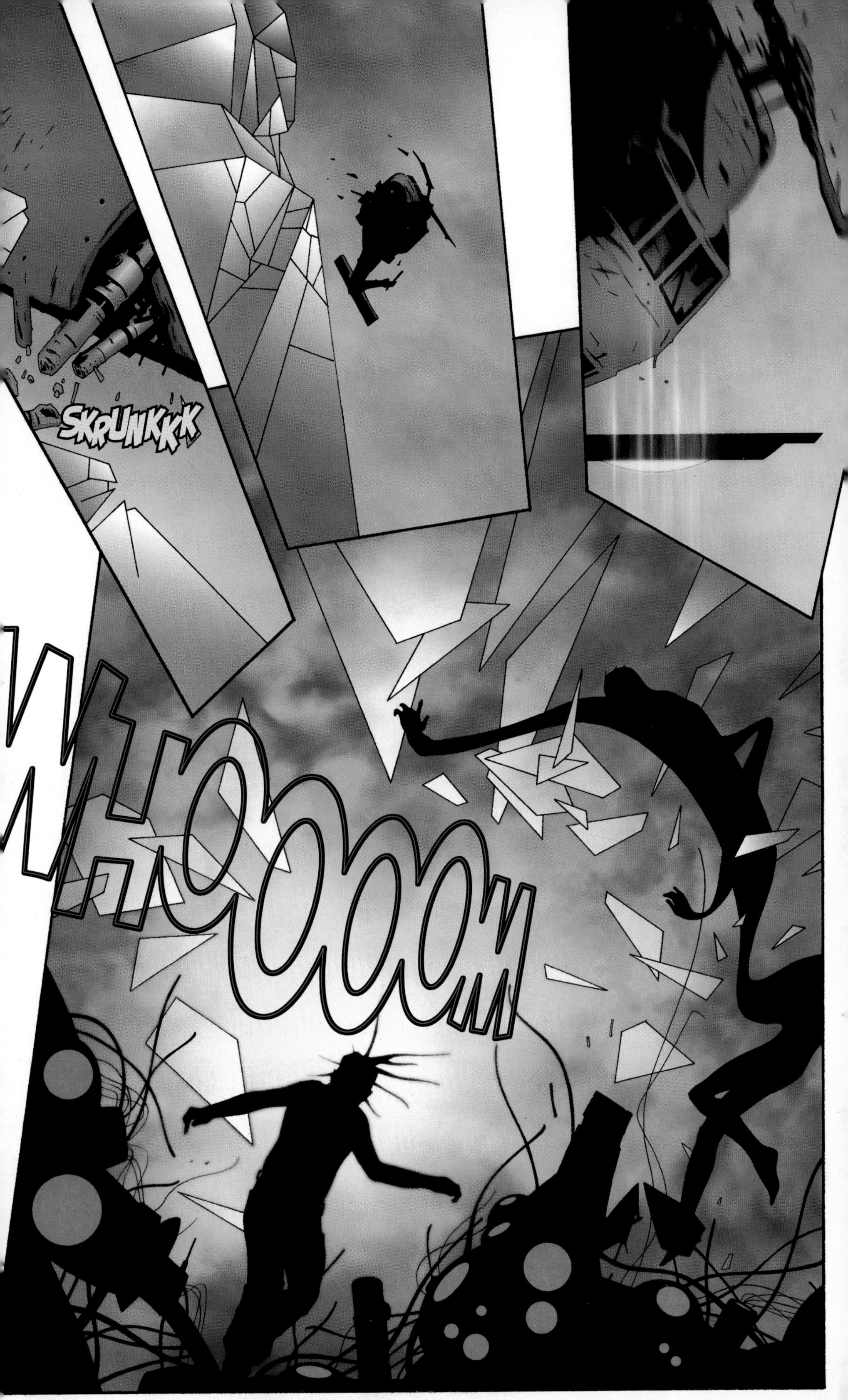
SKRUNKKK
WHOOOOM

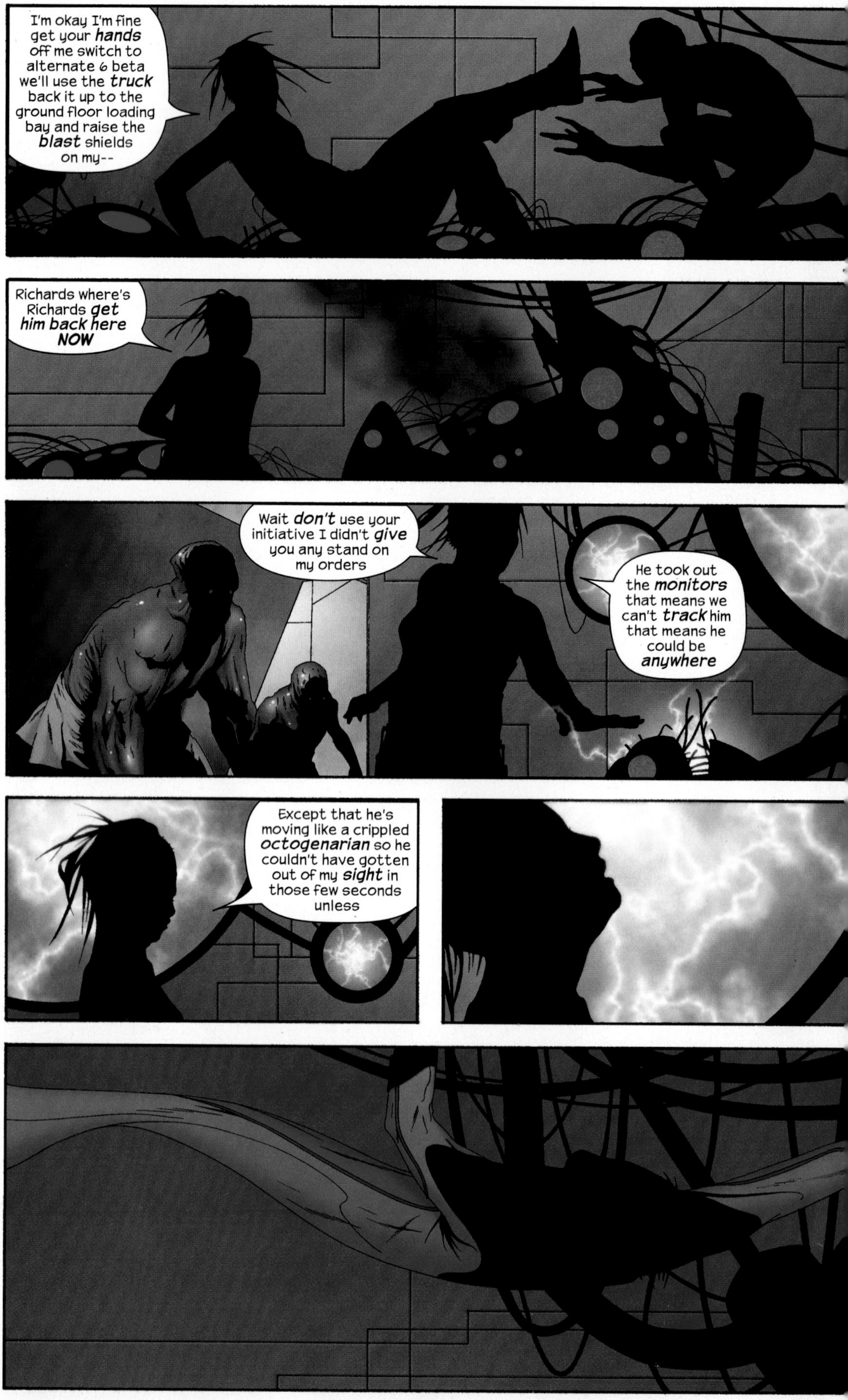
I'm okay I'm fine get your *hands* off me switch to alternate 6 beta we'll use the *truck* back it up to the ground floor loading bay and raise the *blast* shields on my--
Richards where's Richards *get him back here NOW*
Wait *don't* use your initiative I didn't *give* you any stand on my orders
He took out the *monitors* that means we can't *track* him that means he could be *anywhere*
Except that he's moving like a crippled *octogenarian* so he couldn't have gotten out of my *sight* in those few seconds unless

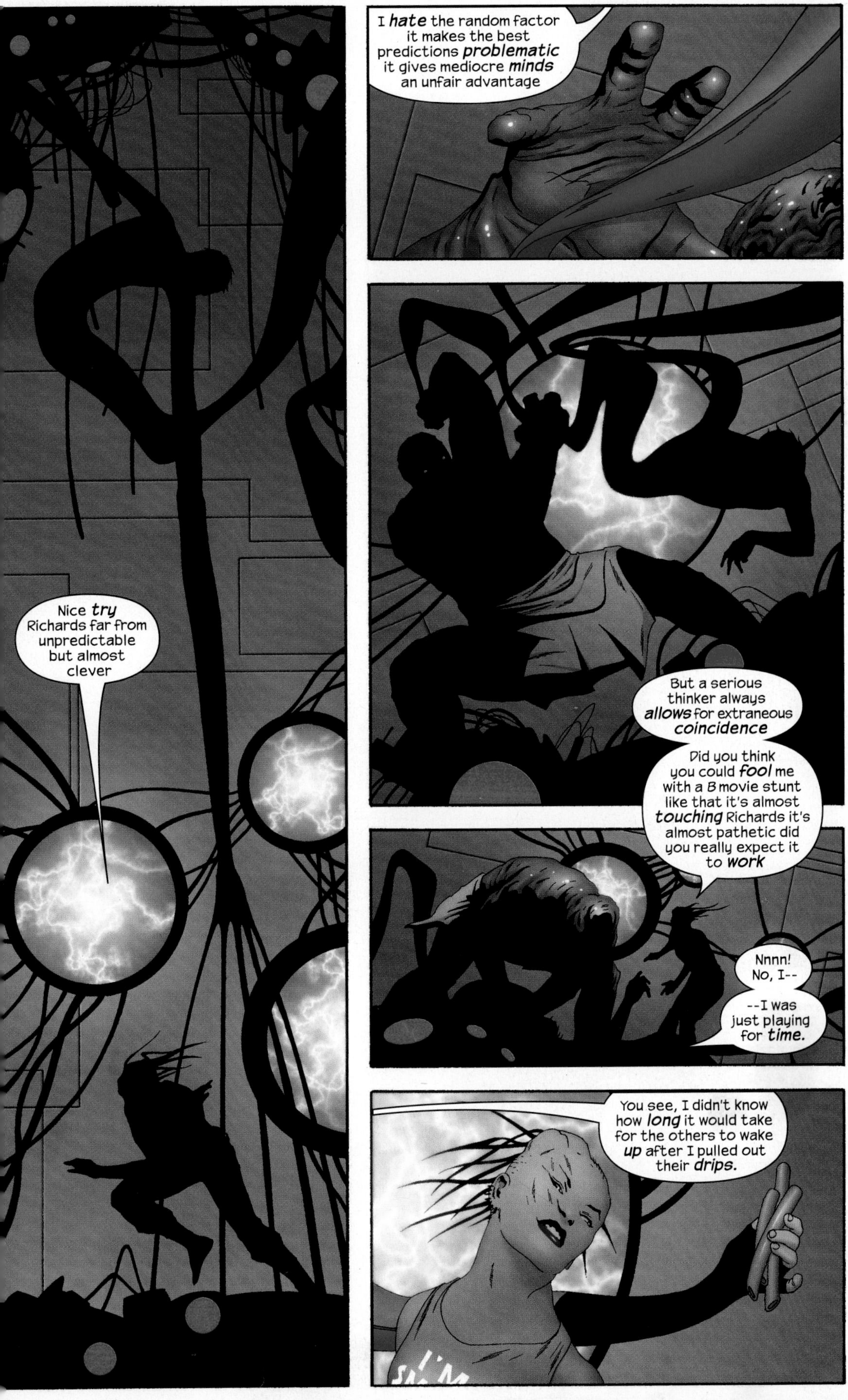
Nice *try* Richards far from unpredictable but almost clever
I *hate* the random factor it makes the best predictions *problematic* it gives mediocre *minds* an unfair advantage
But a serious thinker always *allows* for extraneous *coincidence*
Did you think you could *fool* me with a B movie stunt like that it's almost *touching* Richards it's almost pathetic did you really expect it to *work*
Nnnn! No, I--
--I was just playing for *time.*
You see, I didn't know how *long* it would take for the others to wake *up* after I pulled out their *drips.*
I'M

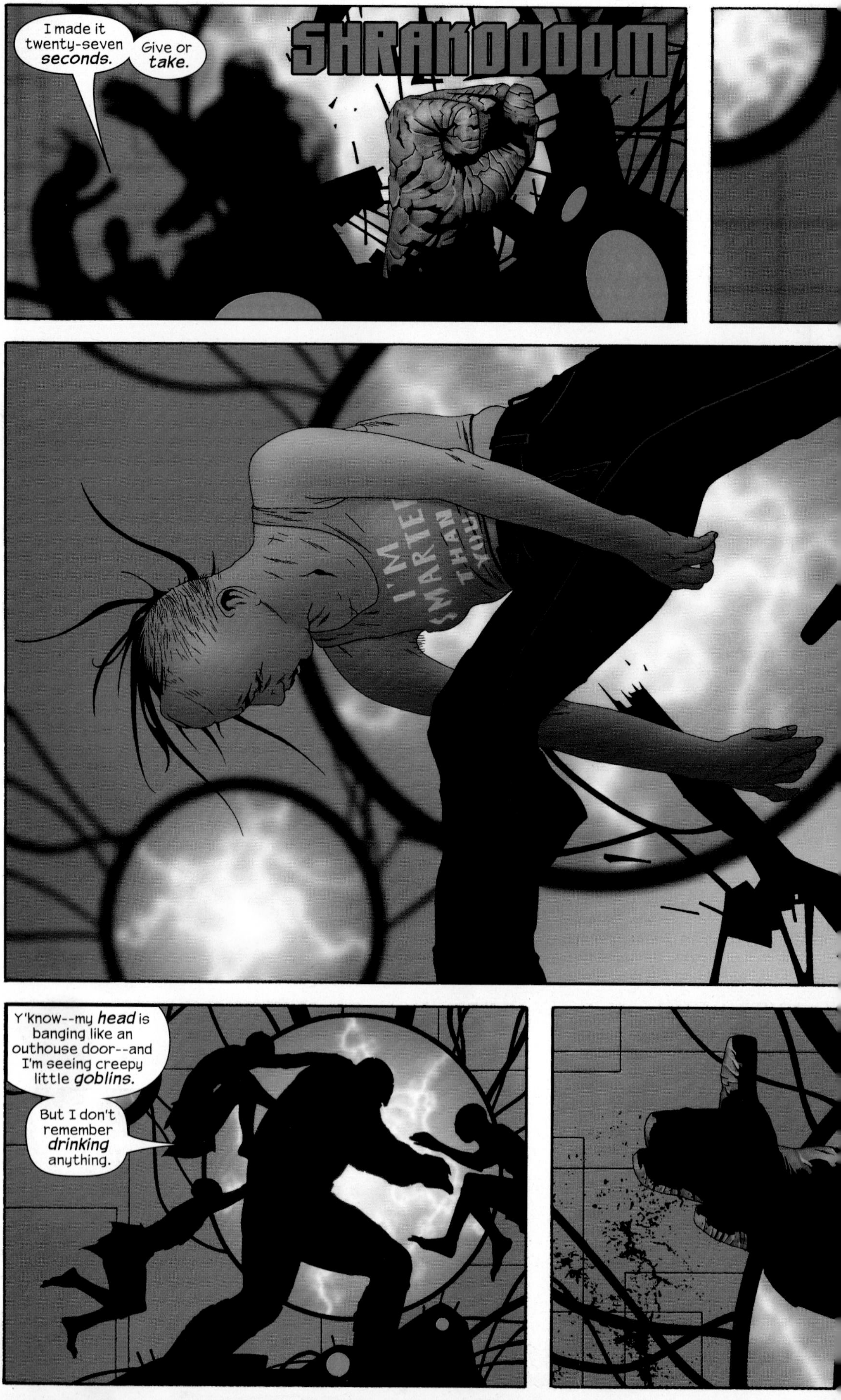
I made it twenty-seven *seconds.*
Give or *take.*
SHRAKOOOOM
I'M SMARTER THAN YOU
Y'know--my *head* is banging like an outhouse door--and I'm seeing creepy little *goblins.*
But I don't remember *drinking* anything.

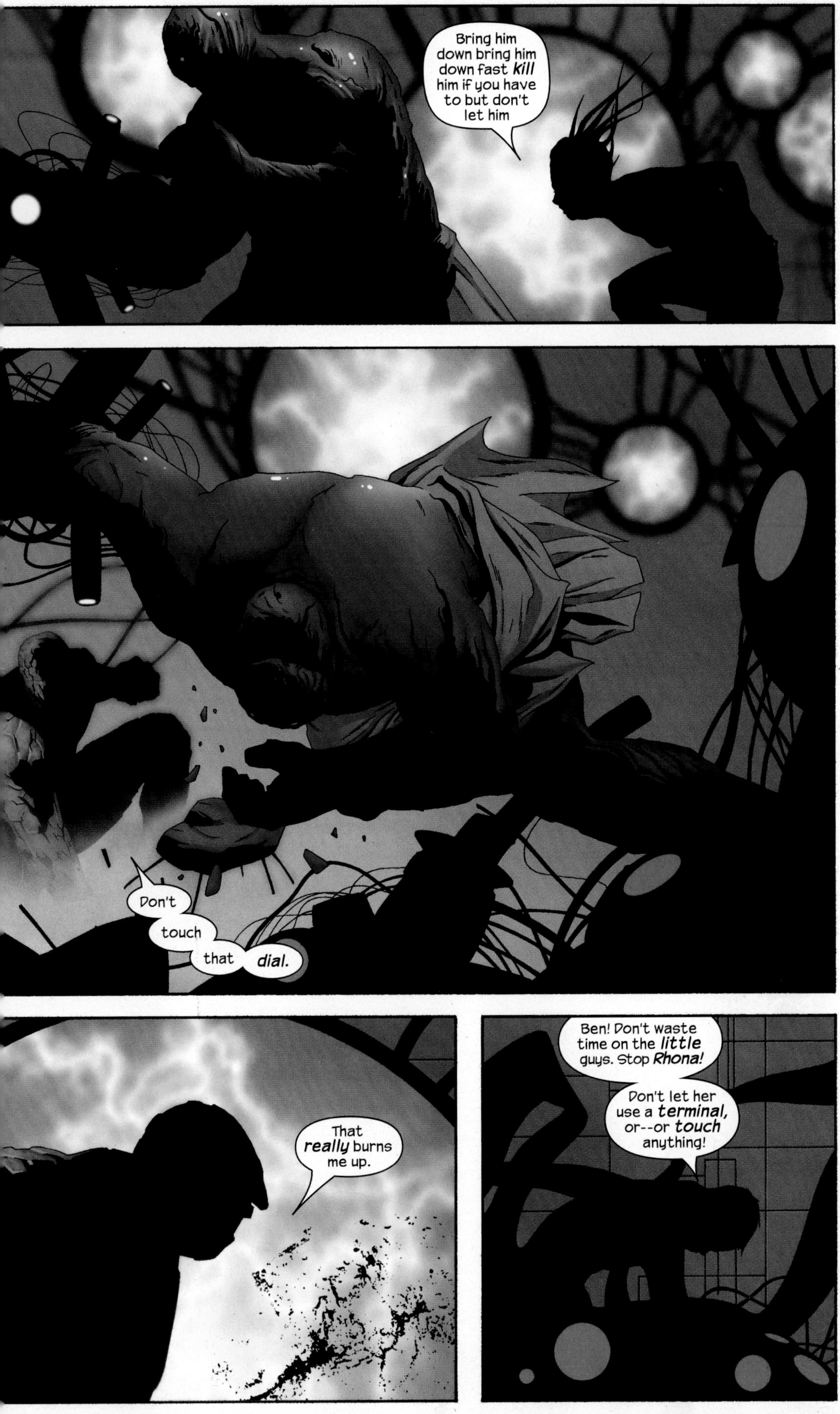
Bring him down bring him down fast kill him if you have to but don't let him
Don't
touch
that
dial.
That really burns me up.
Ben! Don't waste time on the little guys. Stop Rhona!
Don't let her use a terminal, or--or touch anything!

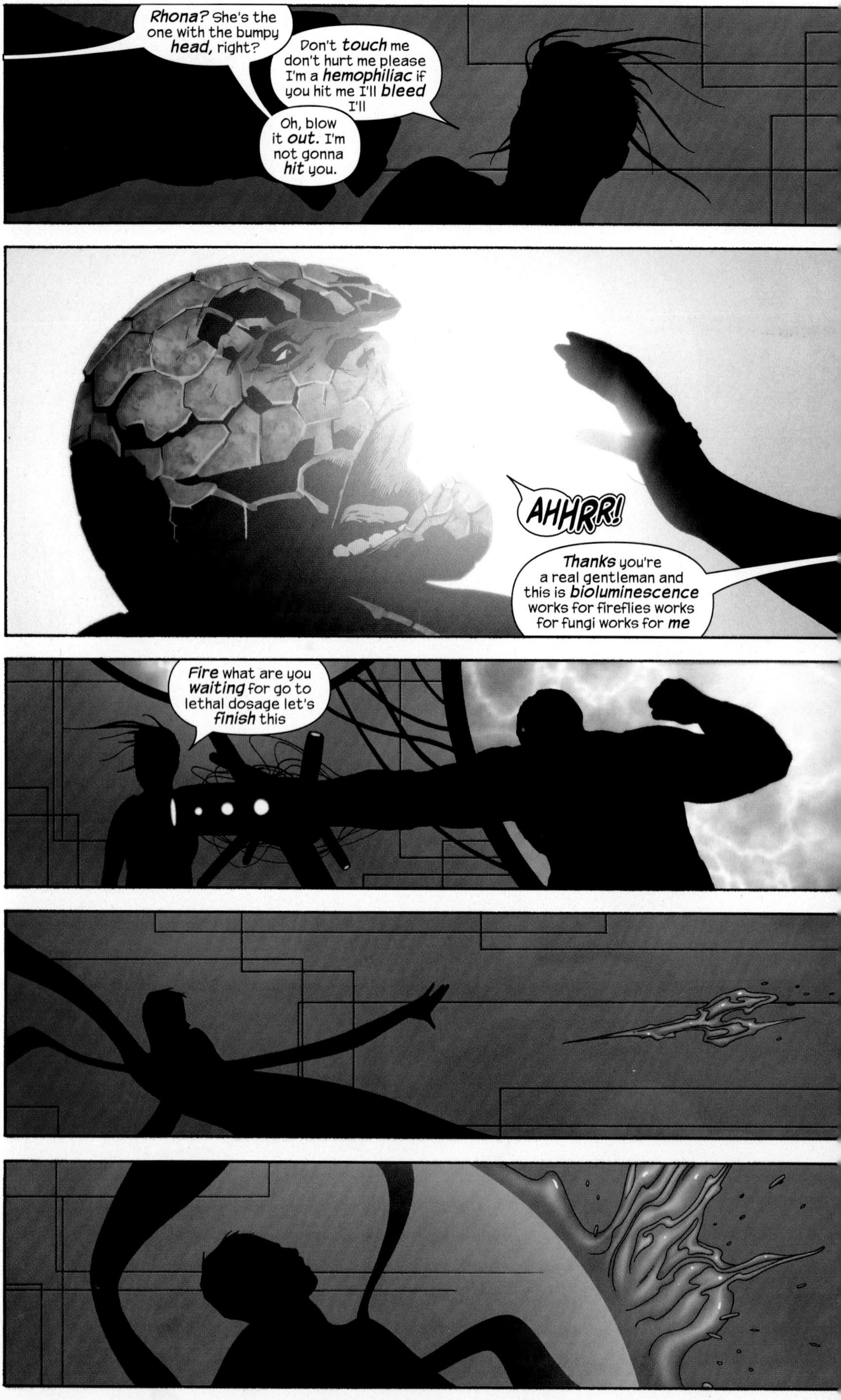
Rhona? She's the one with the bumpy head, right?
Don't touch me don't hurt me please I'm a hemophiliac if you hit me I'll bleed I'll
Oh, blow it out. I'm not gonna hit you.
AHHRR!
Thanks you're a real gentleman and this is bioluminescence works for fireflies works for fungi works for me
Fire what are you waiting for go to lethal dosage let's finish this

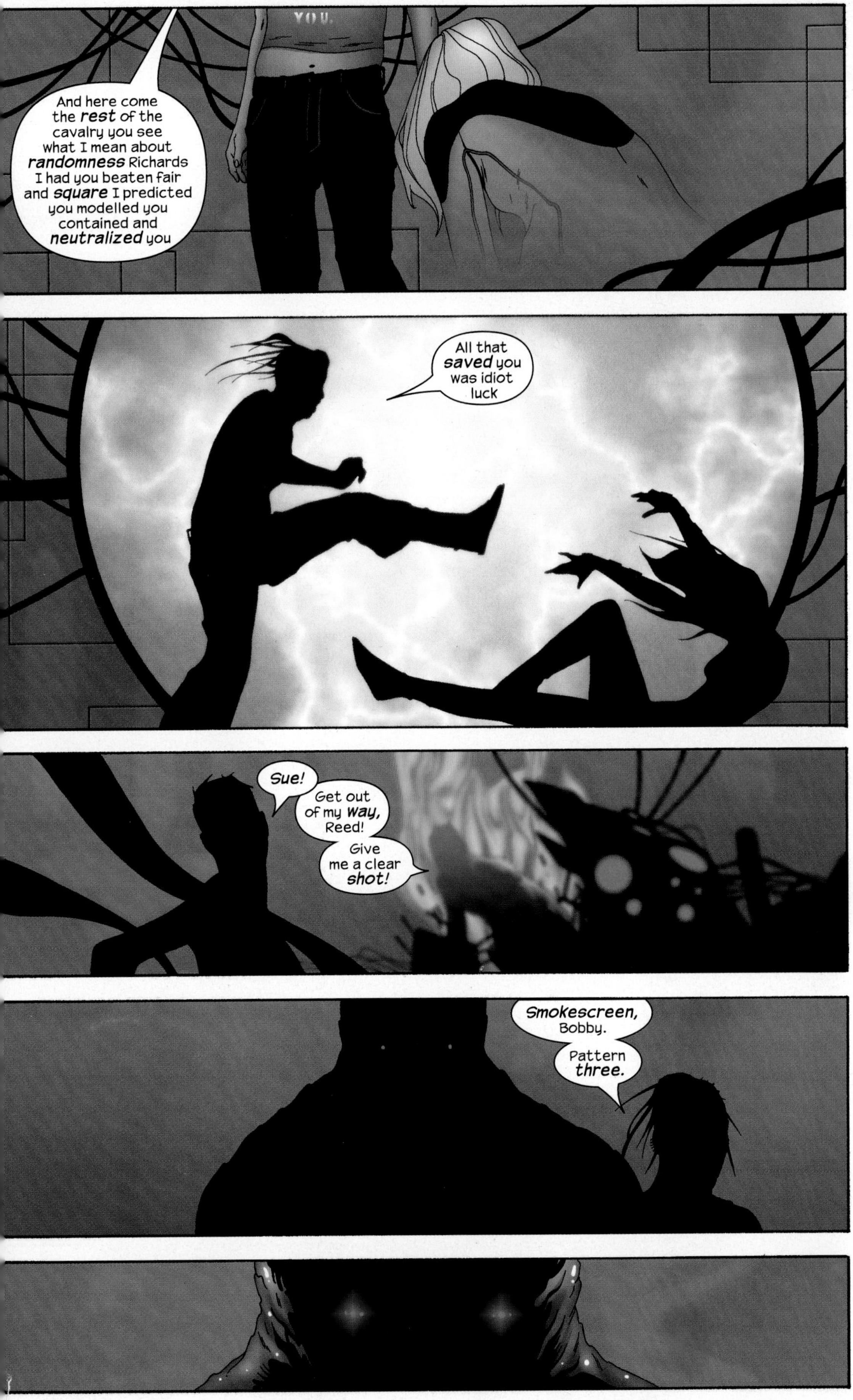

And here come the rest of the cavalry you see what I mean about randomness Richards I had you beaten fair and square I predicted you modelled you contained and neutralized you
All that saved you was idiot luck
Sue!
Get out of my way, Reed!
Give me a clear shot!
Smokescreen, Bobby.
Pattern three.

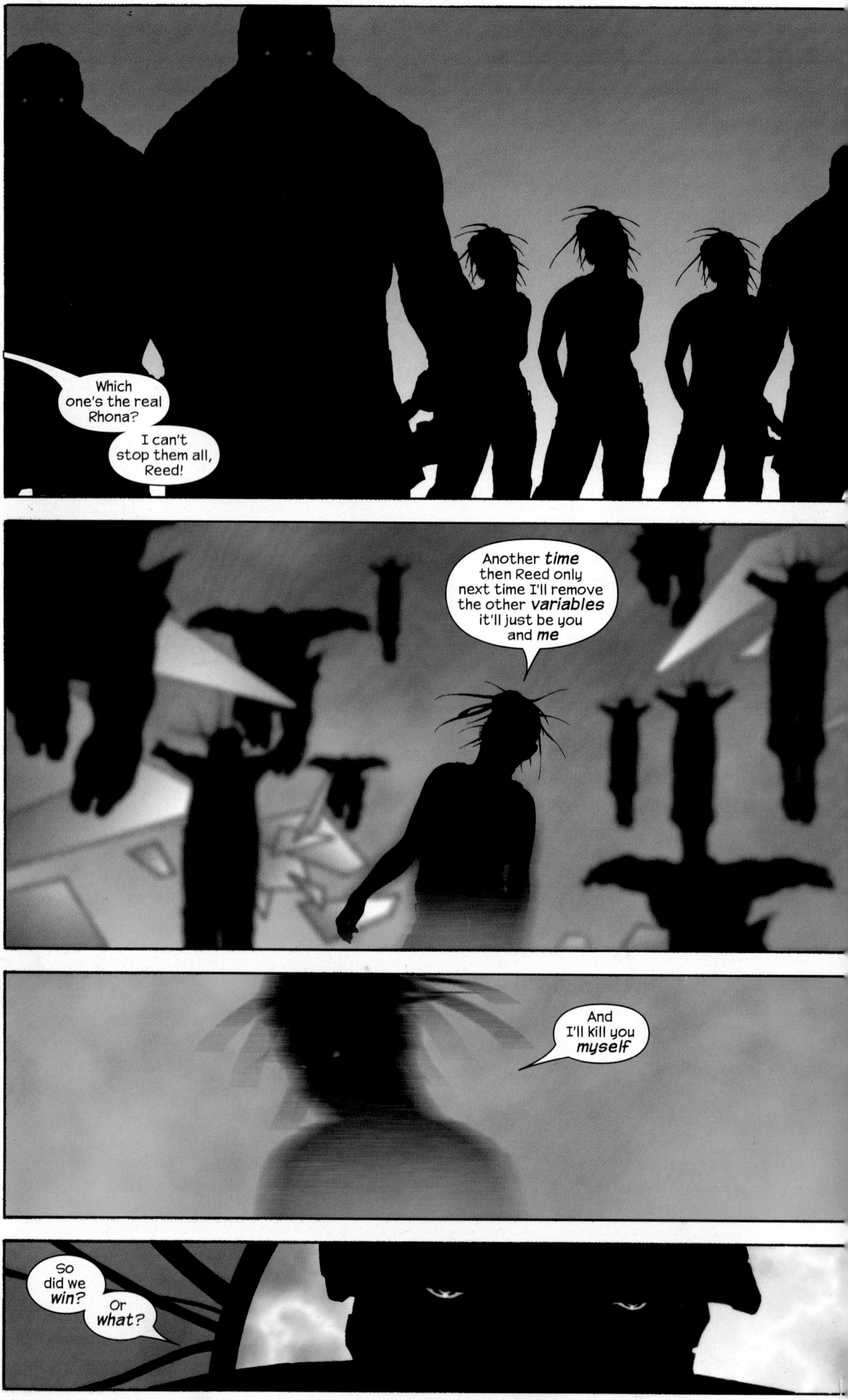
Which one's the real Rhona?
I can't stop them all, Reed!
Another *time* then Reed only next time I'll remove the other *variables* it'll just be you and *me*
And I'll kill you *myself*
So did we *win?*
Or *what?*

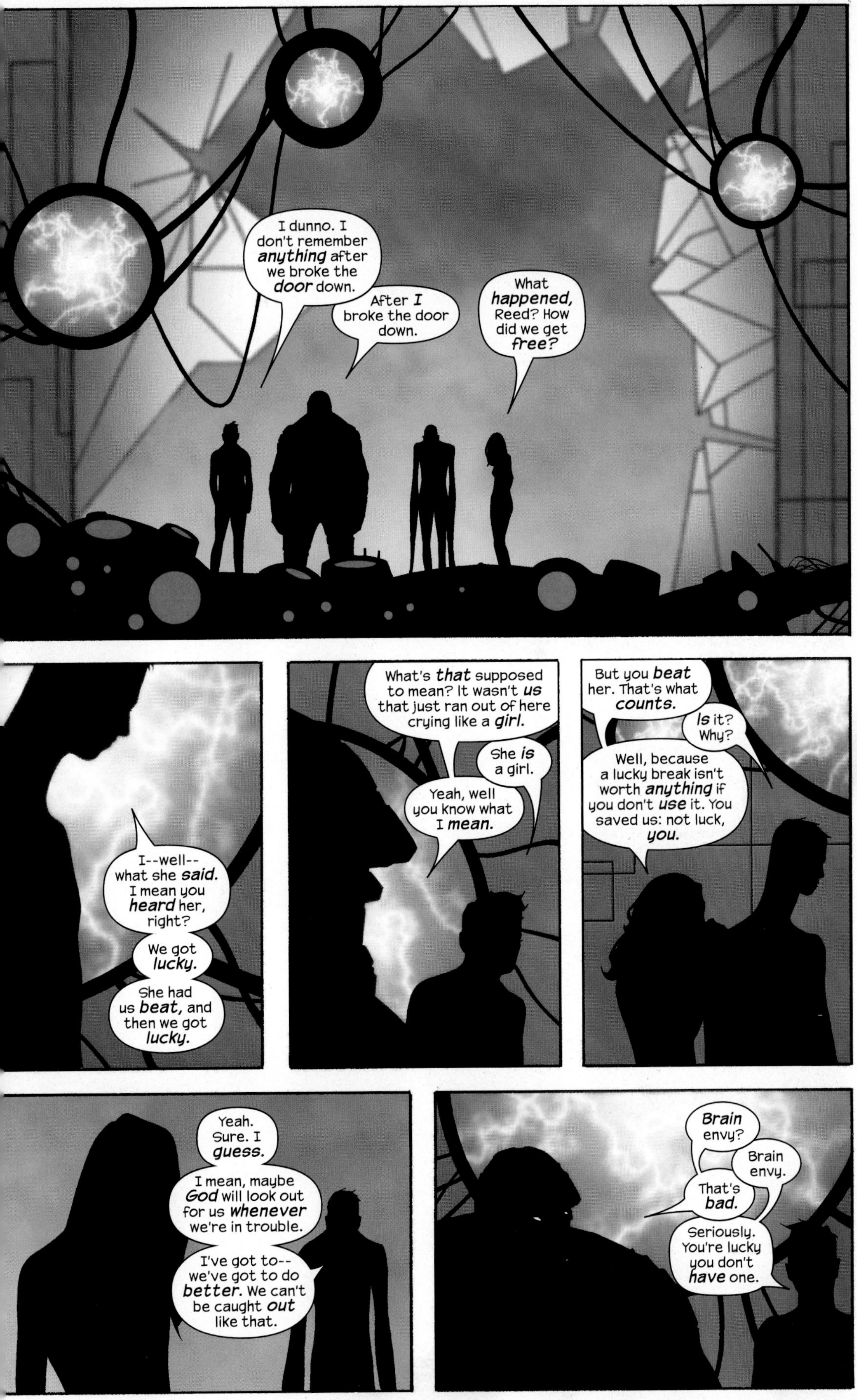
I dunno. I don't remember anything after we broke the door down.
After I broke the door down.
What happened, Reed? How did we get free?
I--well--what she said. I mean you heard her, right?
We got lucky.
She had us beat, and then we got lucky.
What's that supposed to mean? It wasn't us that just ran out of here crying like a girl.
She is a girl.
Yeah, well you know what I mean.
But you beat her. That's what counts.
Is it? Why?
Well, because a lucky break isn't worth anything if you don't use it. You saved us: not luck, you.
Yeah. Sure. I guess.
I mean, maybe God will look out for us whenever we're in trouble.
I've got to--we've got to do better. We can't be caught out like that.
Brain envy?
Brain envy.
That's bad.
Seriously. You're lucky you don't have one.

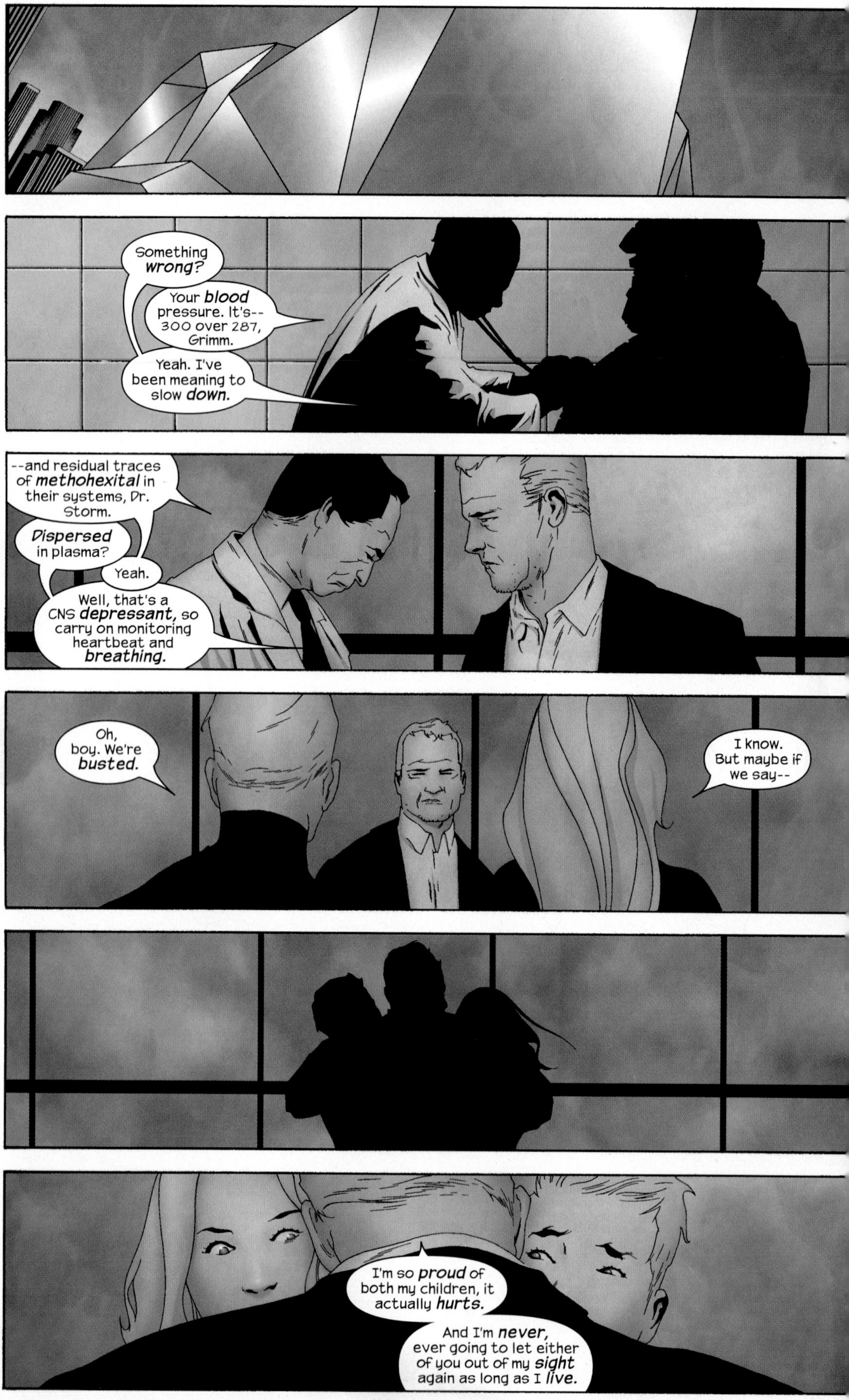

Something *wrong?*
Your *blood* pressure. It's-- 300 over 287, Grimm.
Yeah. I've been meaning to slow *down.*
--and residual traces of *methohexital* in their systems, Dr. Storm.
*Dispersed* in plasma?
Yeah.
Well, that's a CNS *depressant,* so carry on monitoring heartbeat and *breathing.*
Oh, boy. We're *busted.*
I know. But maybe if we say--
I'm so *proud* of both my children, it actually *hurts.*
And I'm *never,* ever going to let either of you out of my *sight* again as long as I *live.*

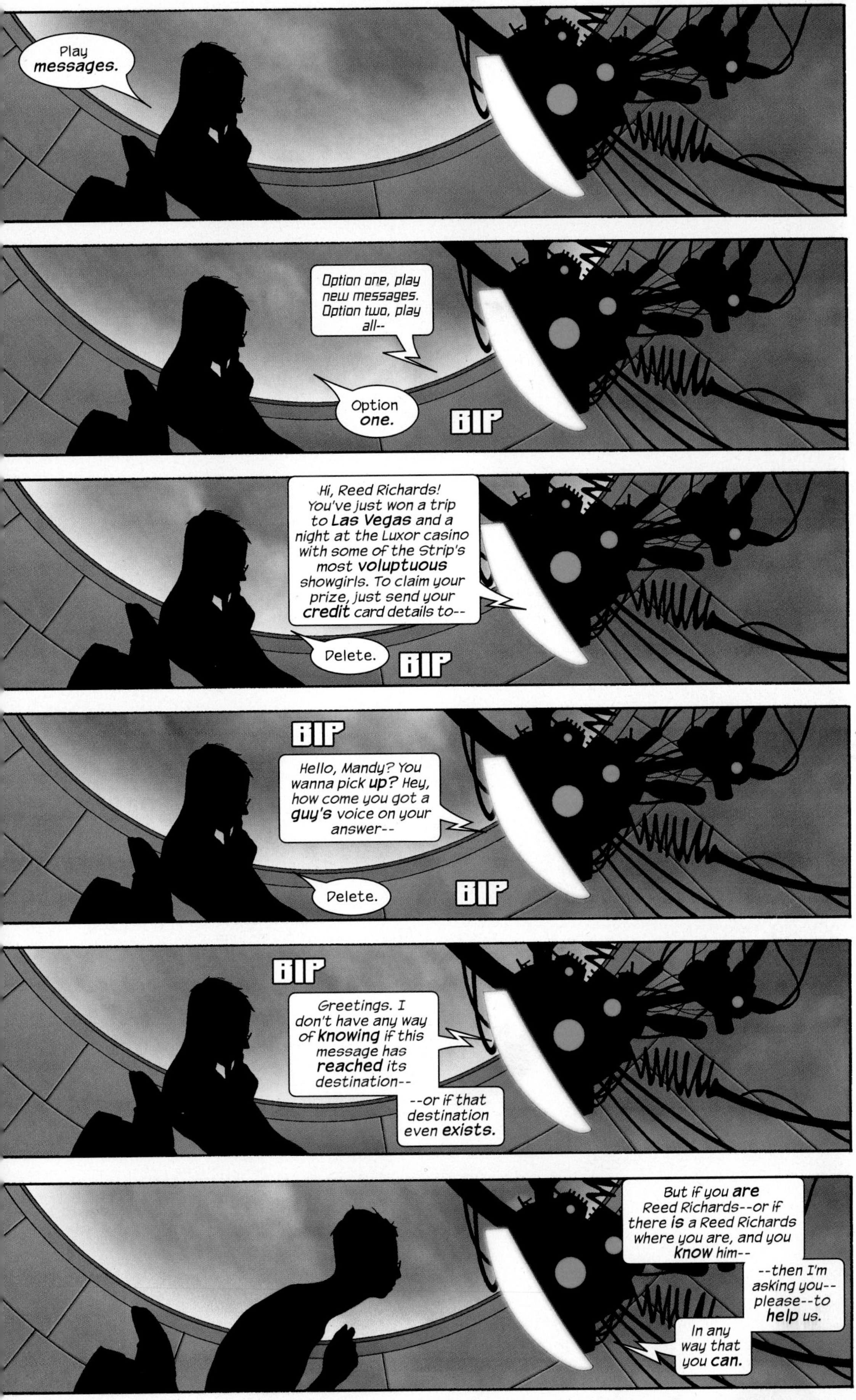
Play messages.
Option one, play new messages. Option two, play all--
Option one.
BIP
Hi, Reed Richards! You've just won a trip to Las Vegas and a night at the Luxor casino with some of the Strip's most voluptuous showgirls. To claim your prize, just send your credit card details to--
Delete.
BIP
BIP
Hello, Mandy? You wanna pick up? Hey, how come you got a guy's voice on your answer--
Delete.
BIP
BIP
Greetings. I don't have any way of knowing if this message has reached its destination--
--or if that destination even exists.
But if you are Reed Richards--or if there is a Reed Richards where you are, and you know him--
--then I'm asking you--please--to help us.
In any way that you can.

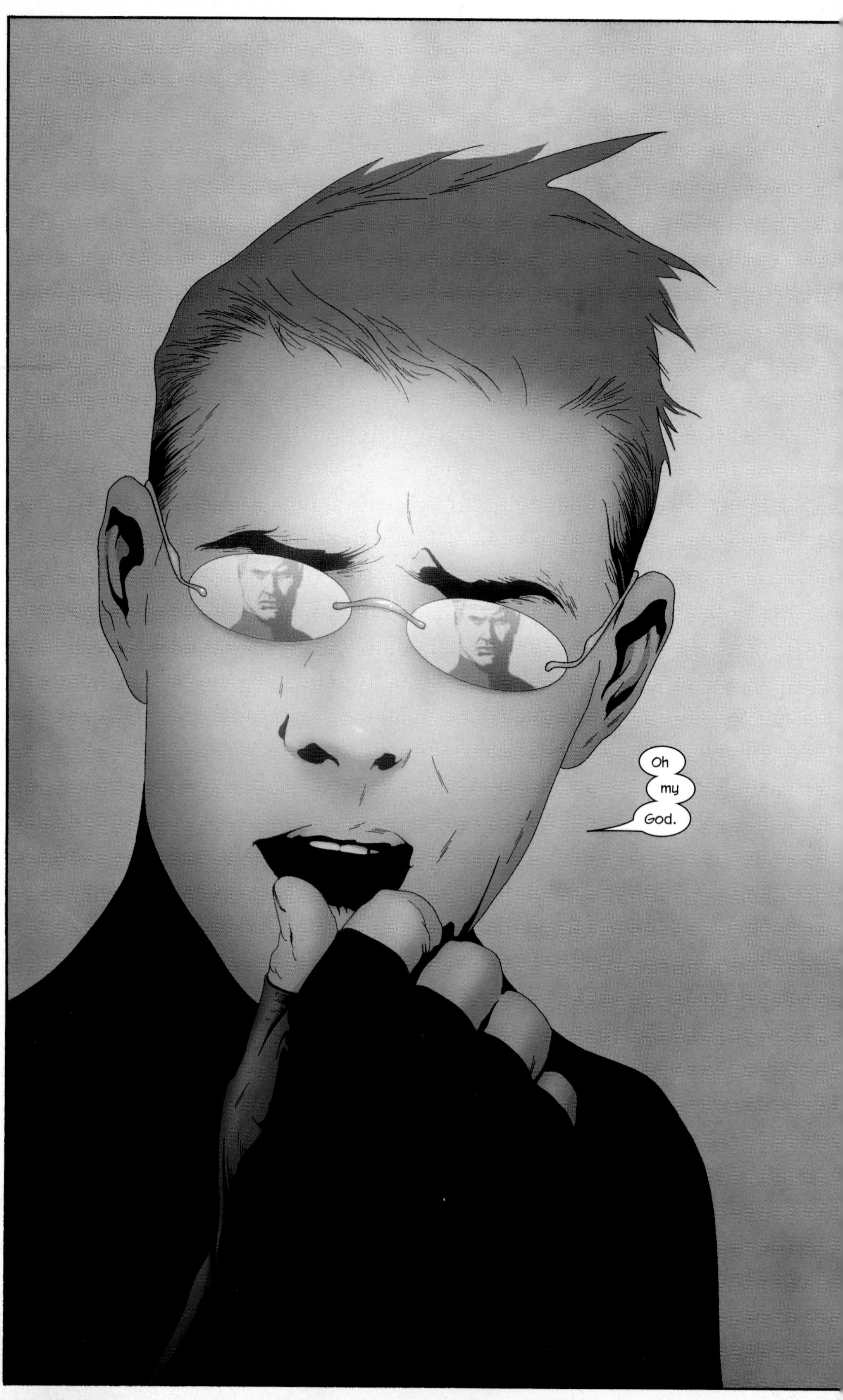
Oh
my
God.

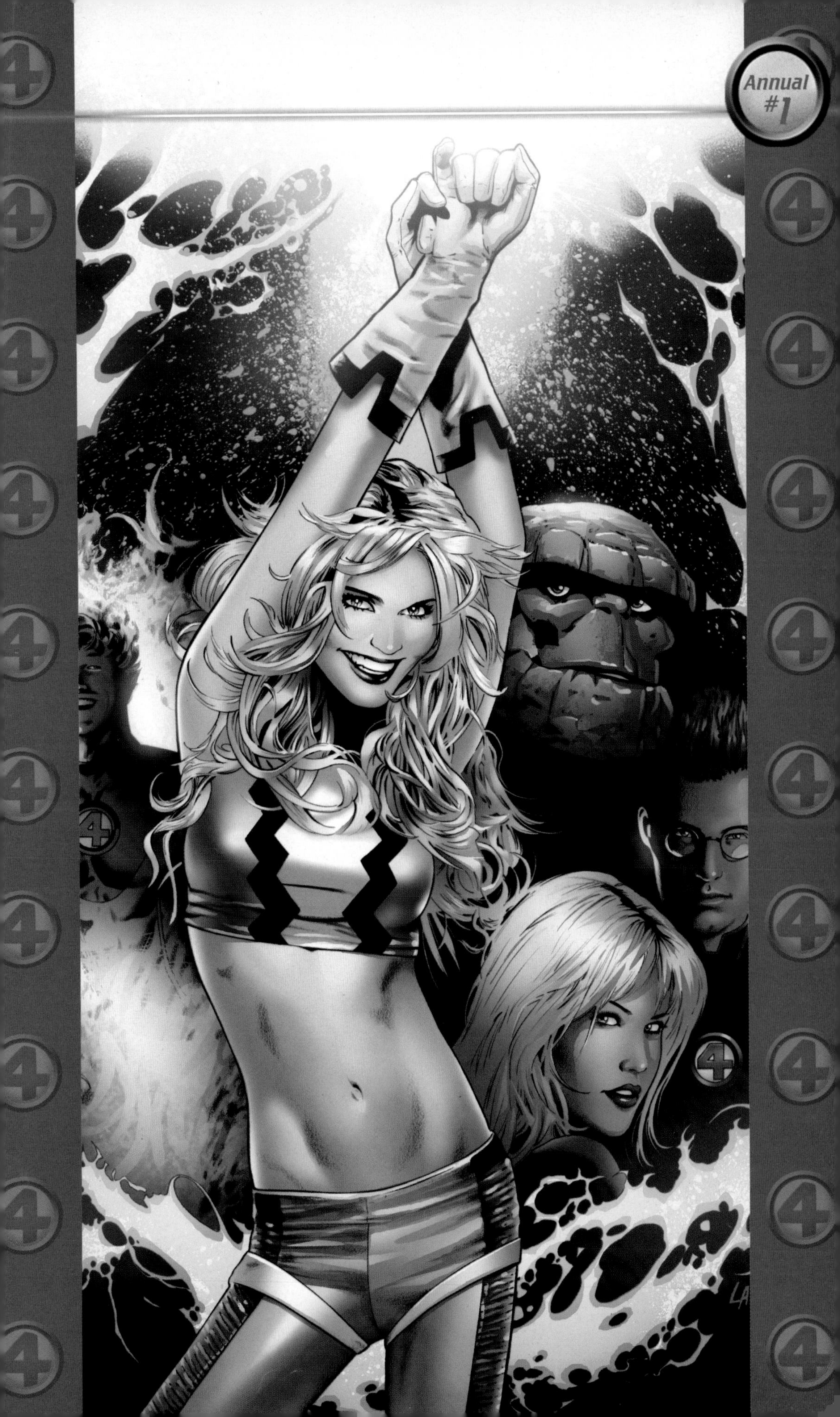
Annual
#1

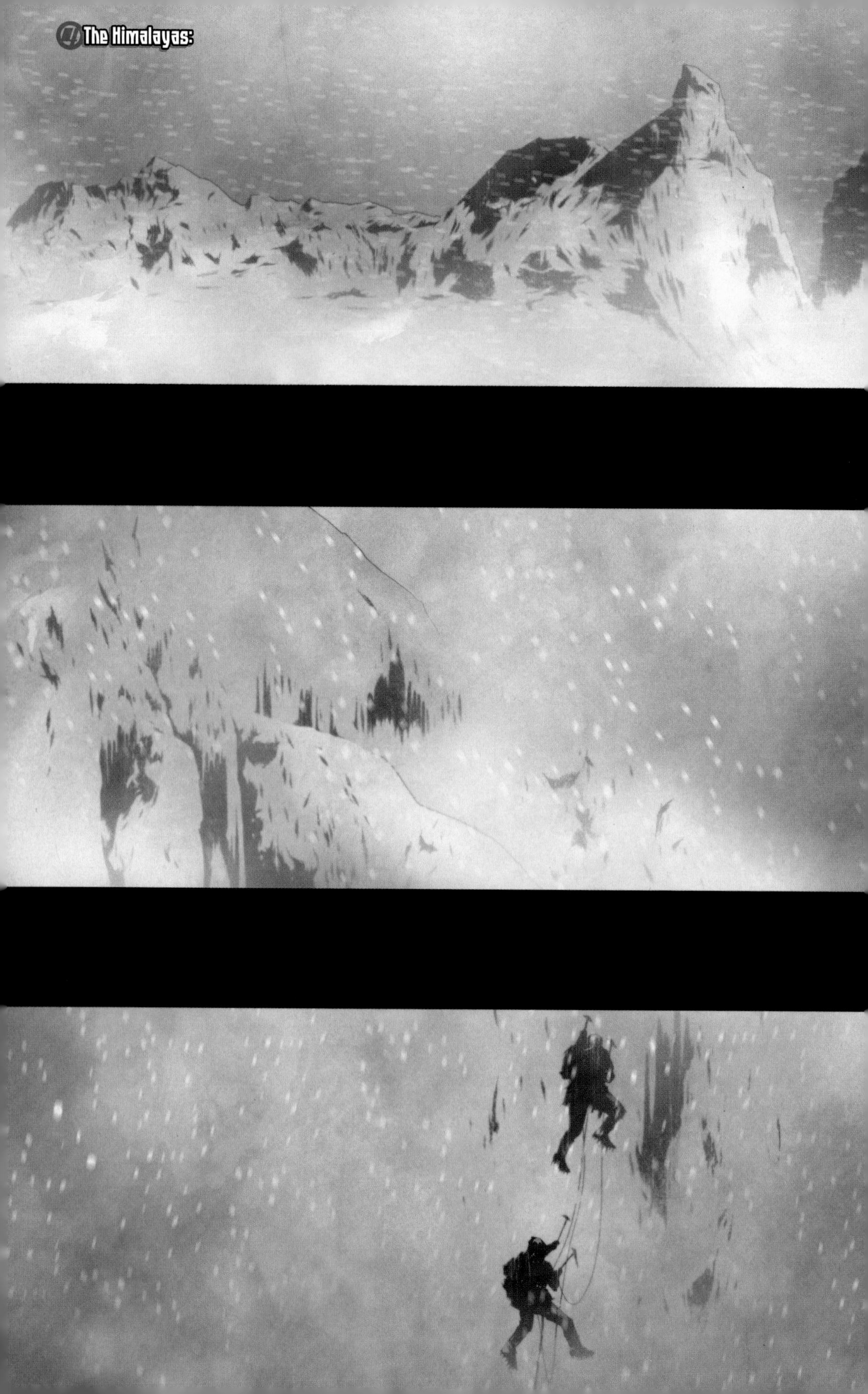
The Himalayas:

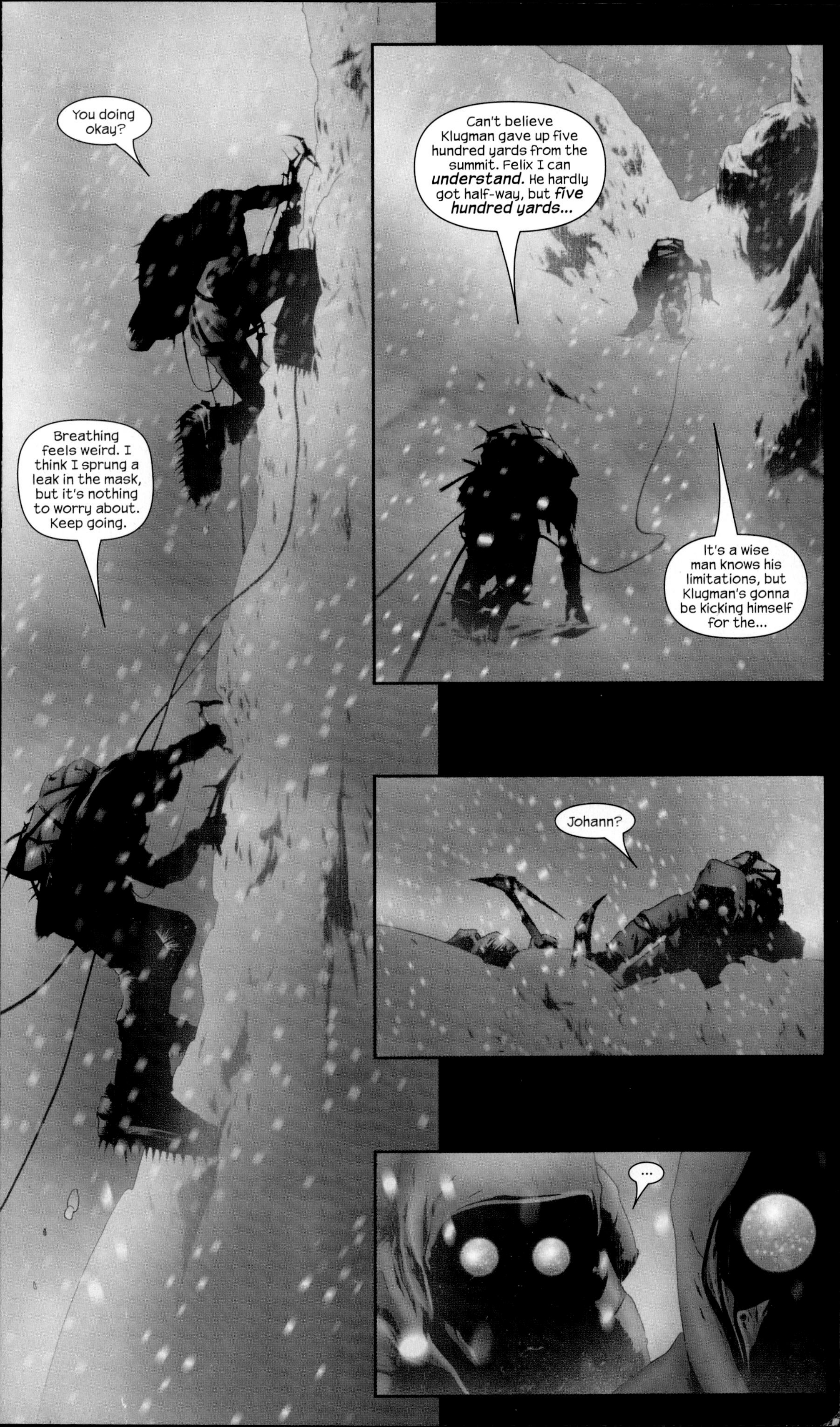

You doing okay?
Breathing feels weird. I think I sprung a leak in the mask, but it's nothing to worry about. Keep going.
Can't believe Klugman gave up five hundred yards from the summit. Felix I can *understand.* He hardly got half-way, but *five hundred yards...*
It's a wise man knows his limitations, but Klugman's gonna be kicking himself for the...
Johann?
...

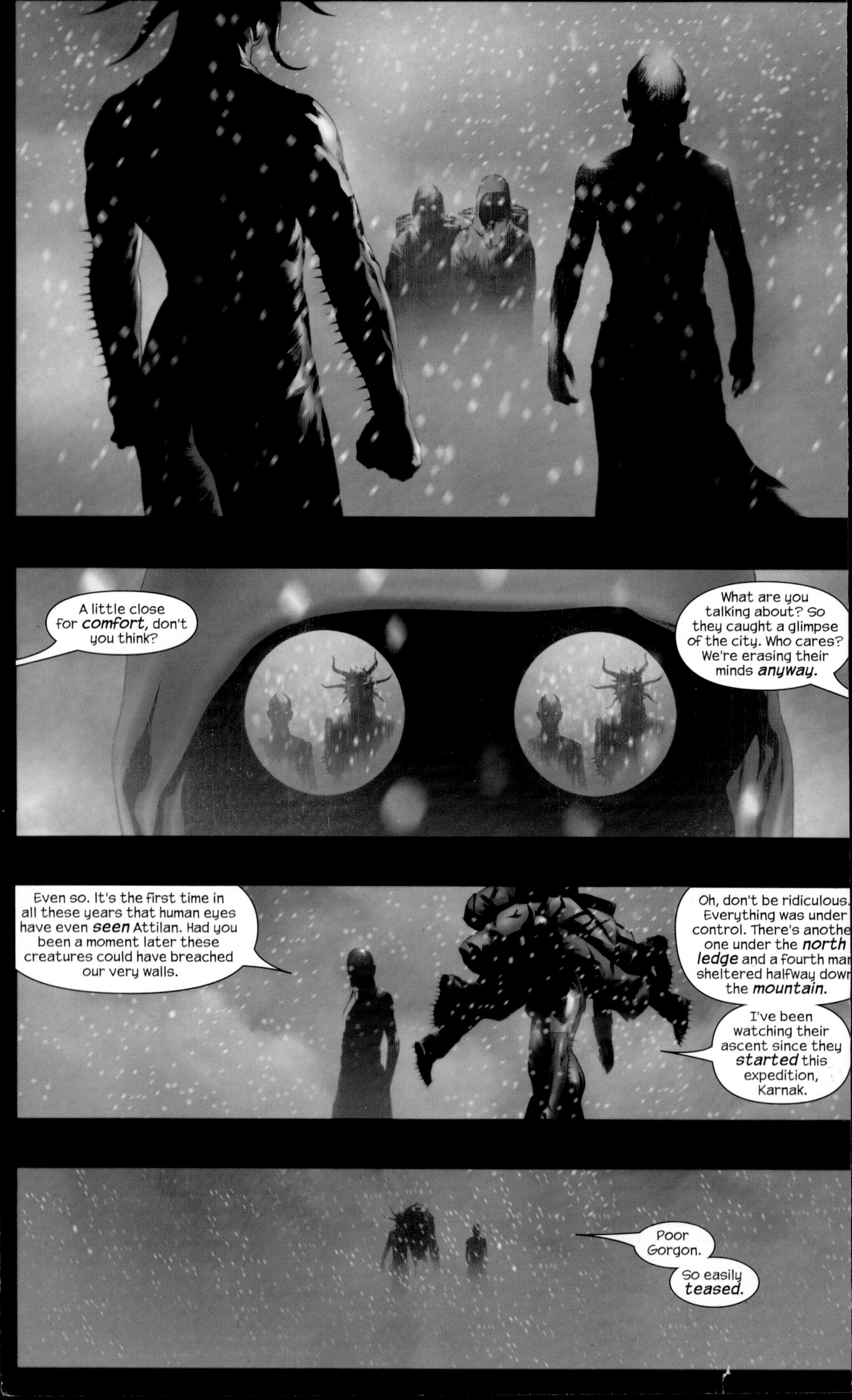
A little close for *comfort*, don't you think?
What are you talking about? So they caught a glimpse of the city. Who cares? We're erasing their minds *anyway.*
Even so. It's the first time in all these years that human eyes have even *seen* Attilan. Had you been a moment later these creatures could have breached our very walls.
Oh, don't be ridiculous. Everything was under control. There's anothe one under the *north ledge* and a fourth ma sheltered halfway dow the *mountain.*
I've been watching their ascent since they *started* this expedition, Karnak.
Poor Gorgon.
So easily *teased.*

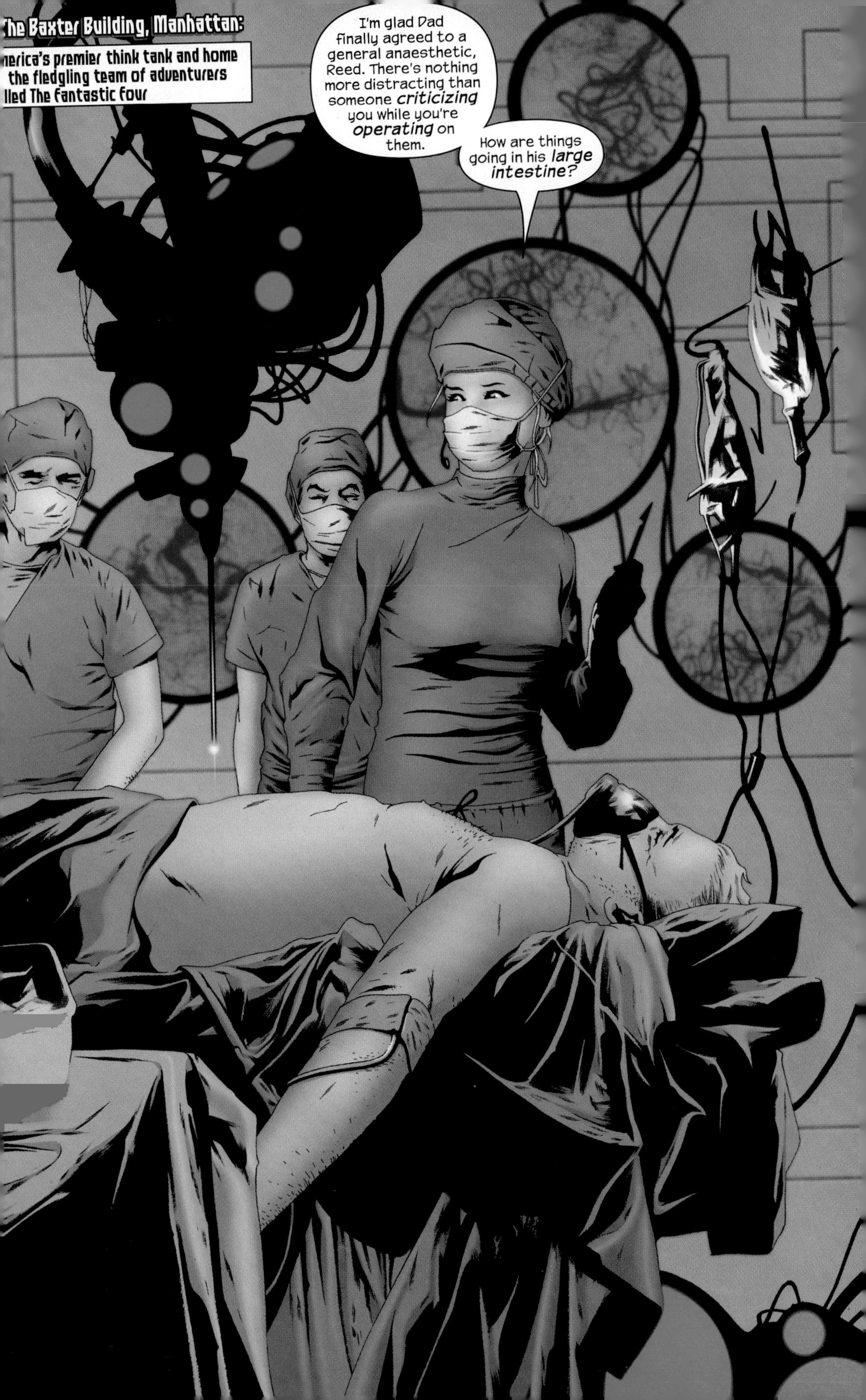
The Baxter Building, Manhattan:
merica's premier think tank and home the fledgling team of adventurers lled The Fantastic Four
I'm glad Dad finally agreed to a general anaesthetic, Reed. There's nothing more distracting than someone criticizing you while you're operating on them.
How are things going in his large intestine?

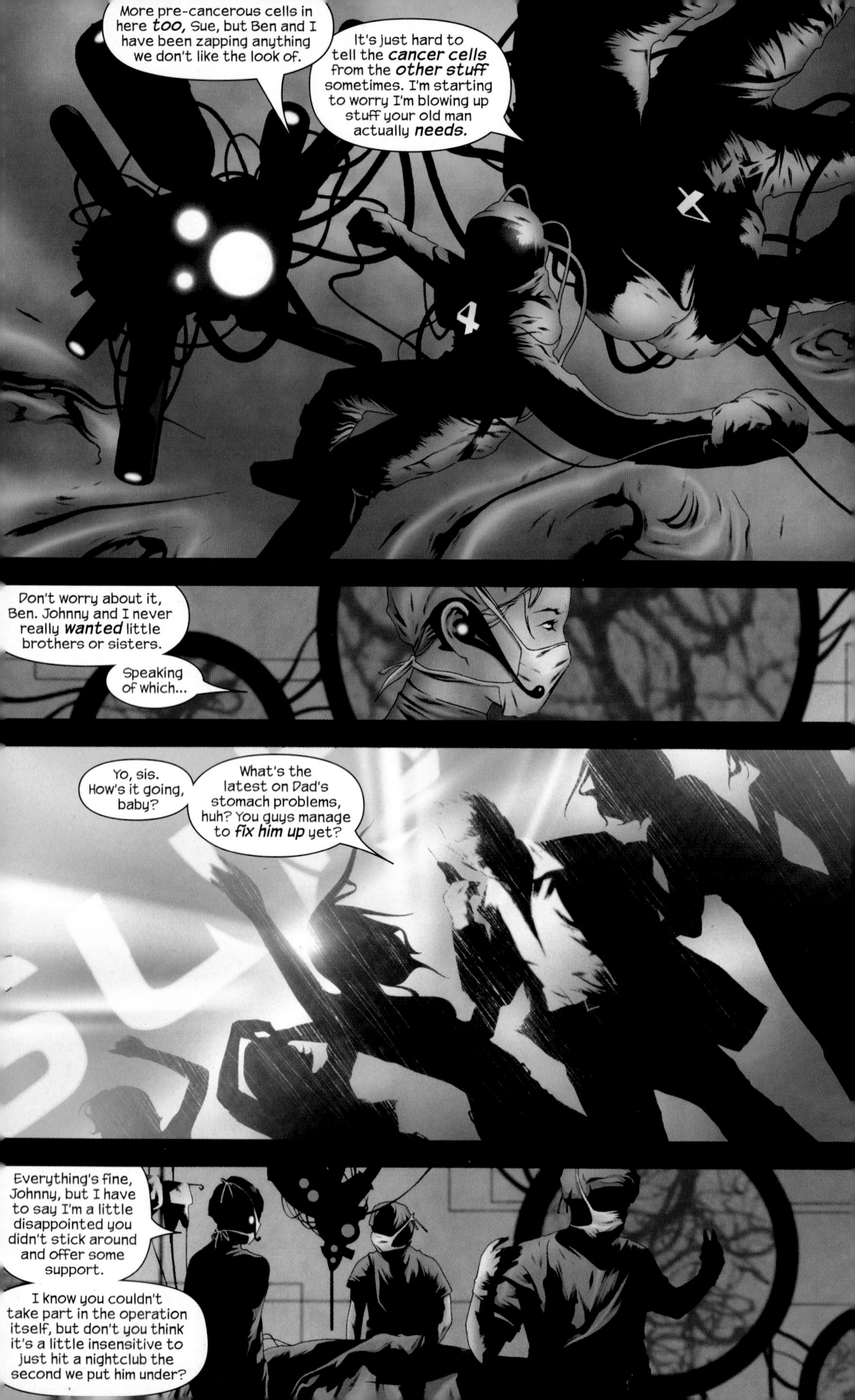
More pre-cancerous cells in here *too,* Sue, but Ben and I have been zapping anything we don't like the look of.
It's just hard to tell the *cancer cells* from the *other stuff* sometimes. I'm starting to worry I'm blowing up stuff your old man actually *needs.*
Don't worry about it, Ben. Johnny and I never really *wanted* little brothers or sisters.
Speaking of which...
Yo, sis. How's it going, baby?
What's the latest on Dad's stomach problems, huh? You guys manage to *fix him up* yet?
Everything's fine, Johnny, but I have to say I'm a little disappointed you didn't stick around and offer some support.
I know you couldn't take part in the operation itself, but don't you think it's a little insensitive to just hit a nightclub the second we put him under?

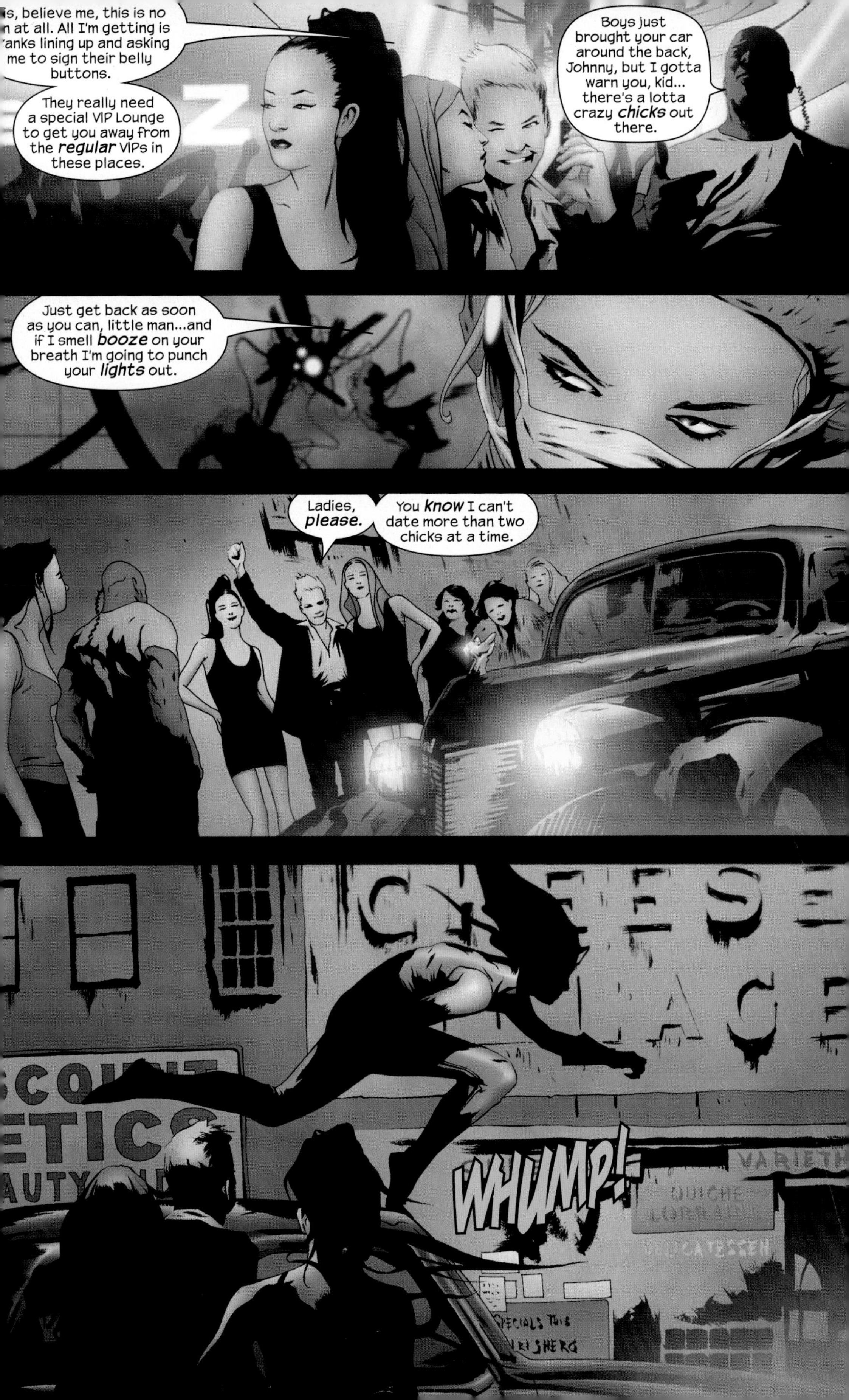
s, believe me, this is no n at all. All I'm getting is ranks lining up and asking me to sign their belly buttons.
They really need a special VIP Lounge to get you away from the regular VIPs in these places.
Boys just brought your car around the back, Johnny, but I gotta warn you, kid... there's a lotta crazy chicks out there.
Just get back as soon as you can, little man...and if I smell booze on your breath I'm going to punch your lights out.
Ladies, please.
You know I can't date more than two chicks at a time.
WHUMP!
QUICHE LORRAINE
DELICATESSEN
SPECIALS THIS

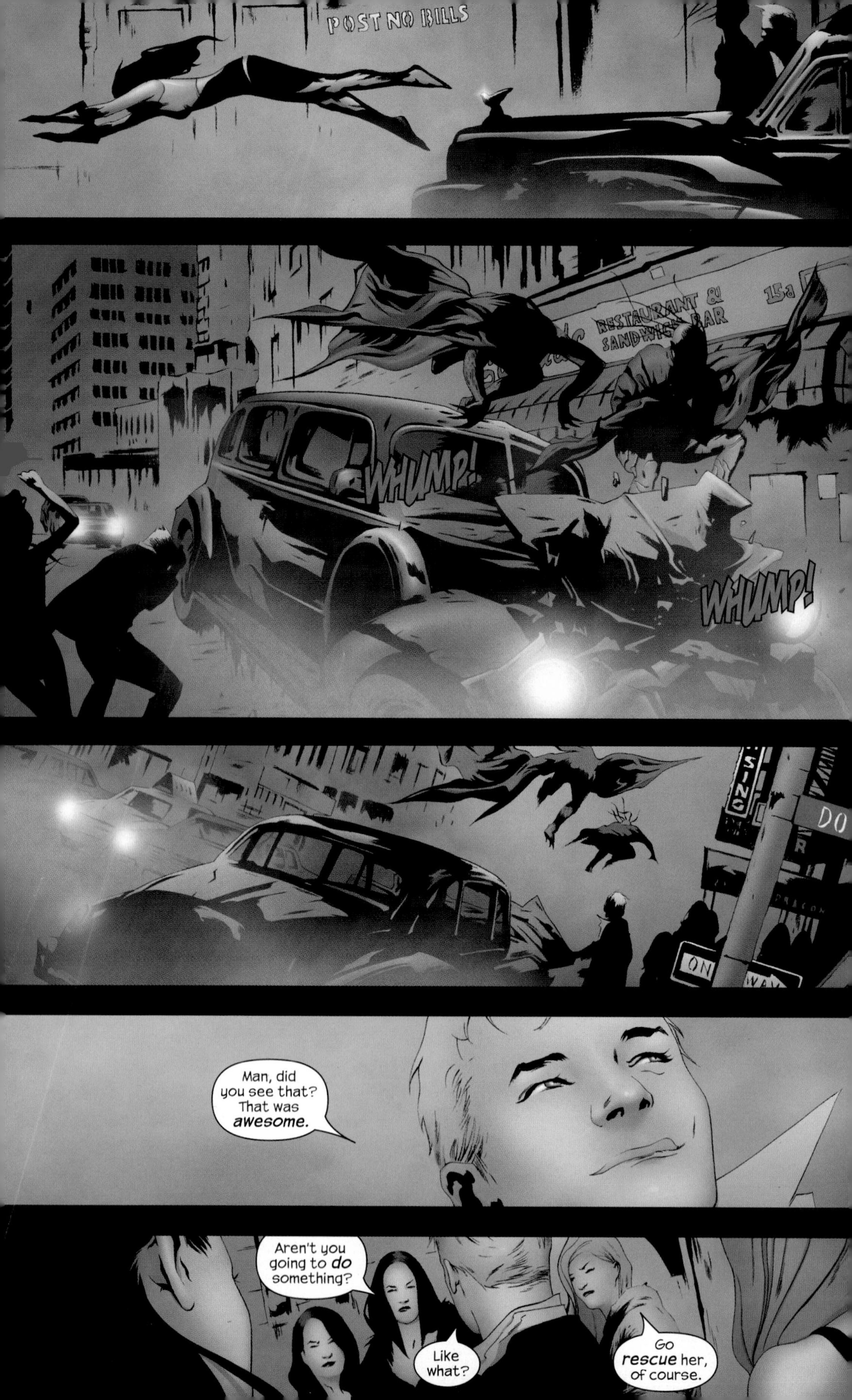
POST NO BILLS
RESTAURANT & SANDWICH BAR
15a
WHUMP!
WHUMP!
Man, did you see that? That was *awesome.*
Aren't you going to *do* something?
Like what?
Go *rescue* her, of course.

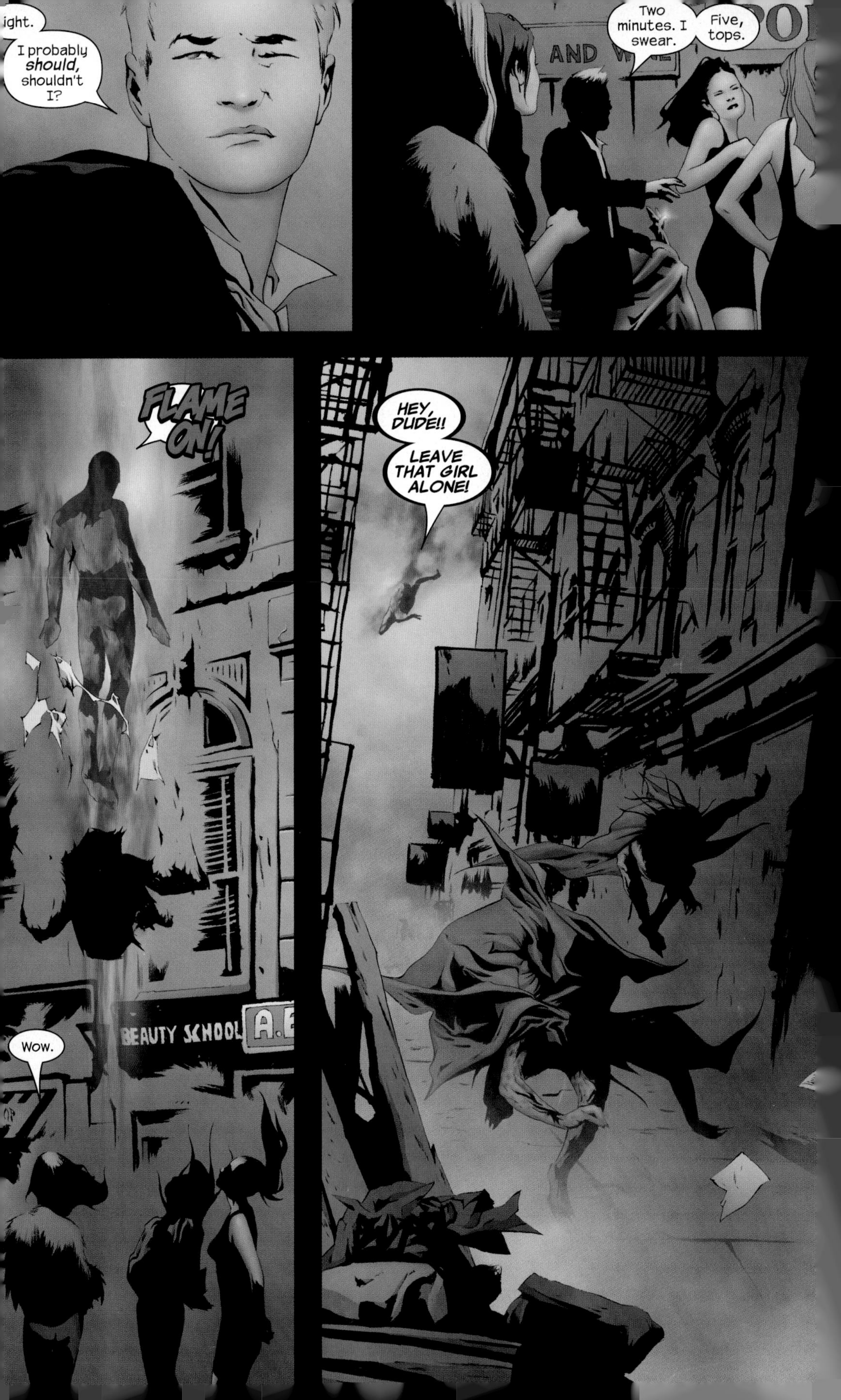

ight.
I probably *should,* shouldn't I?
Two minutes. I swear.
Five, tops.
AND
FLAME ON!
HEY, DUDE!!
LEAVE THAT GIRL ALONE!
BEAUTY SCHOOL
Wow.

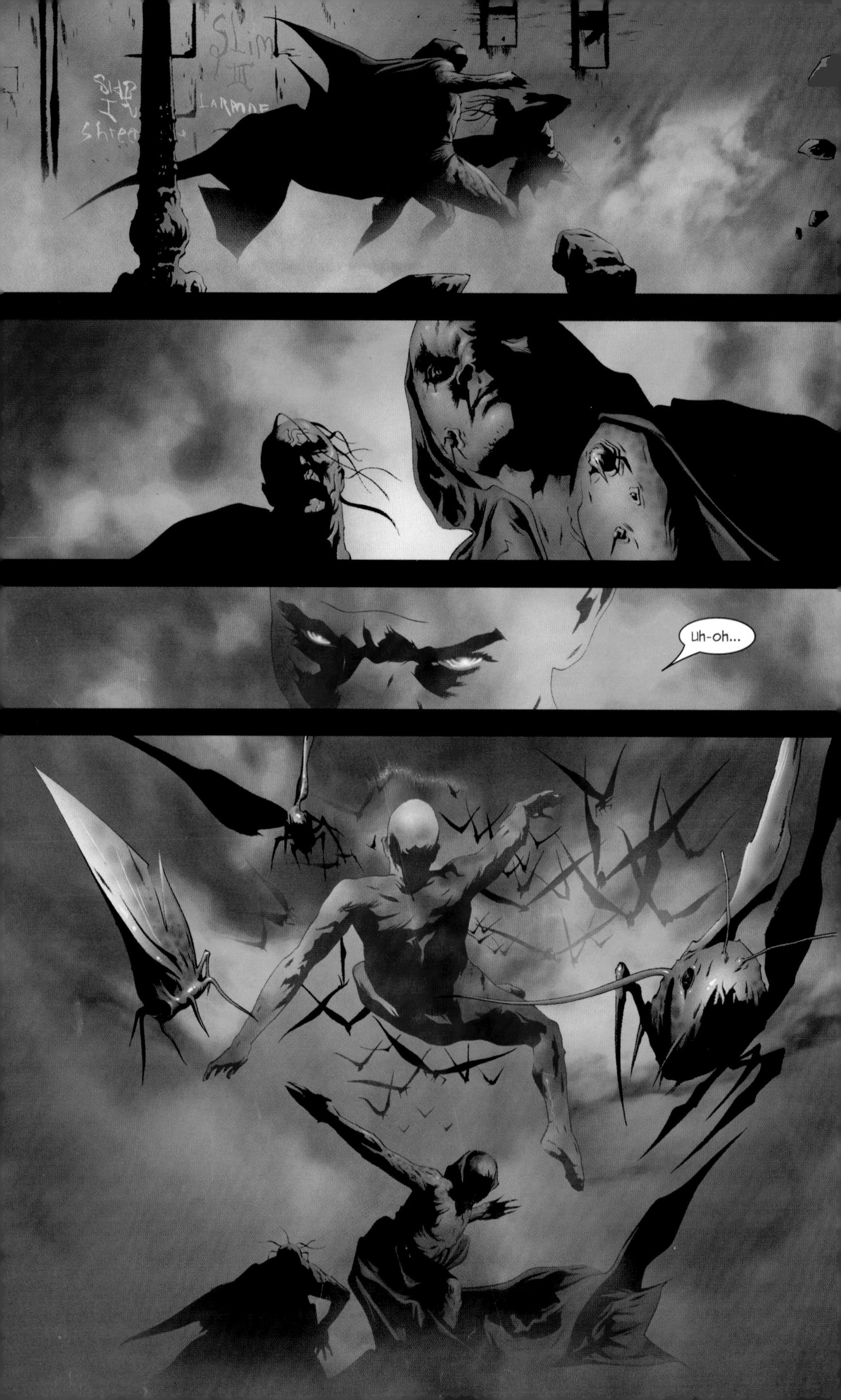
Uh-oh...

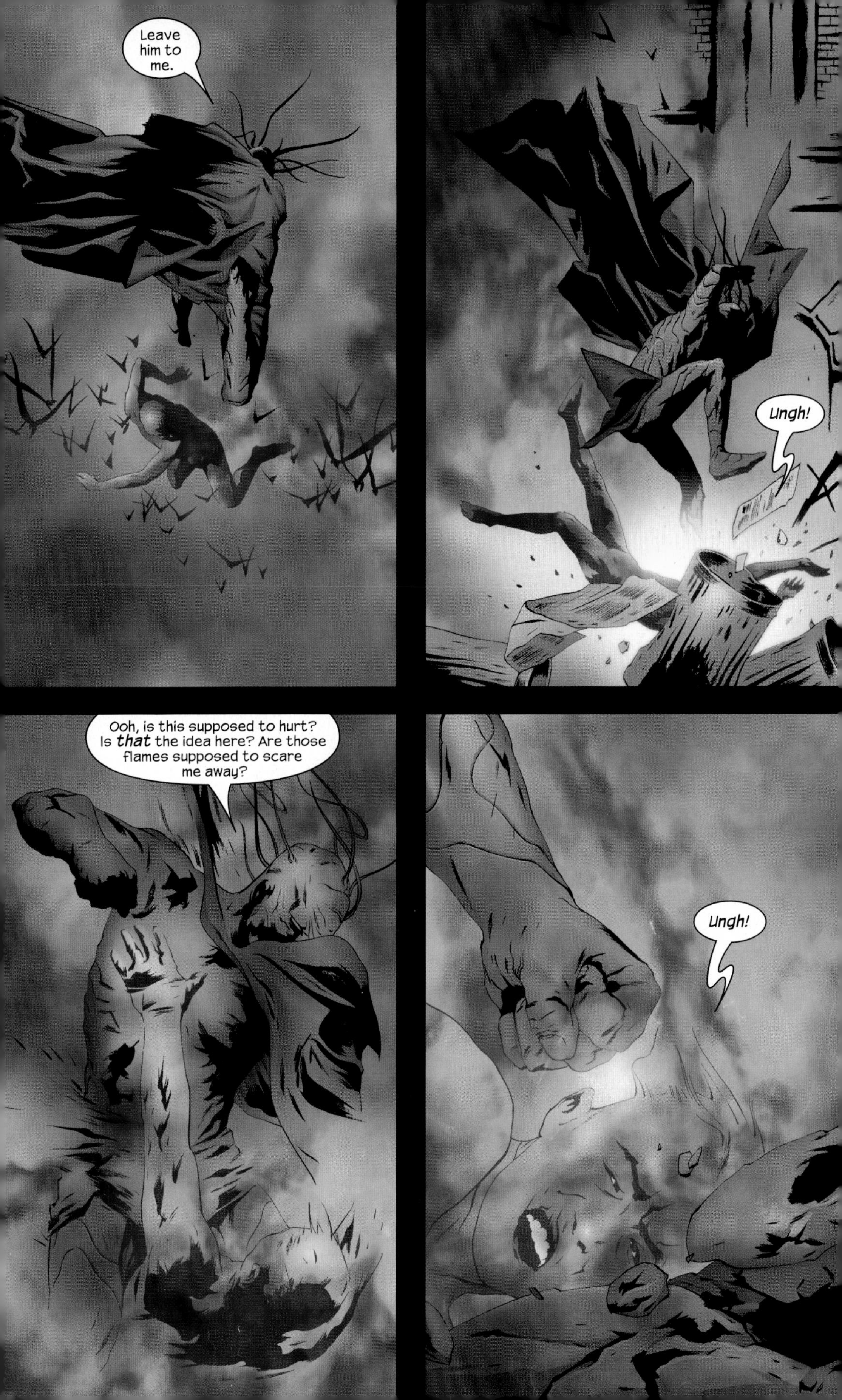
Leave him to me.
Ungh!
Ooh, is this supposed to hurt? Is *that* the idea here? Are those flames supposed to scare me away?
Ungh!

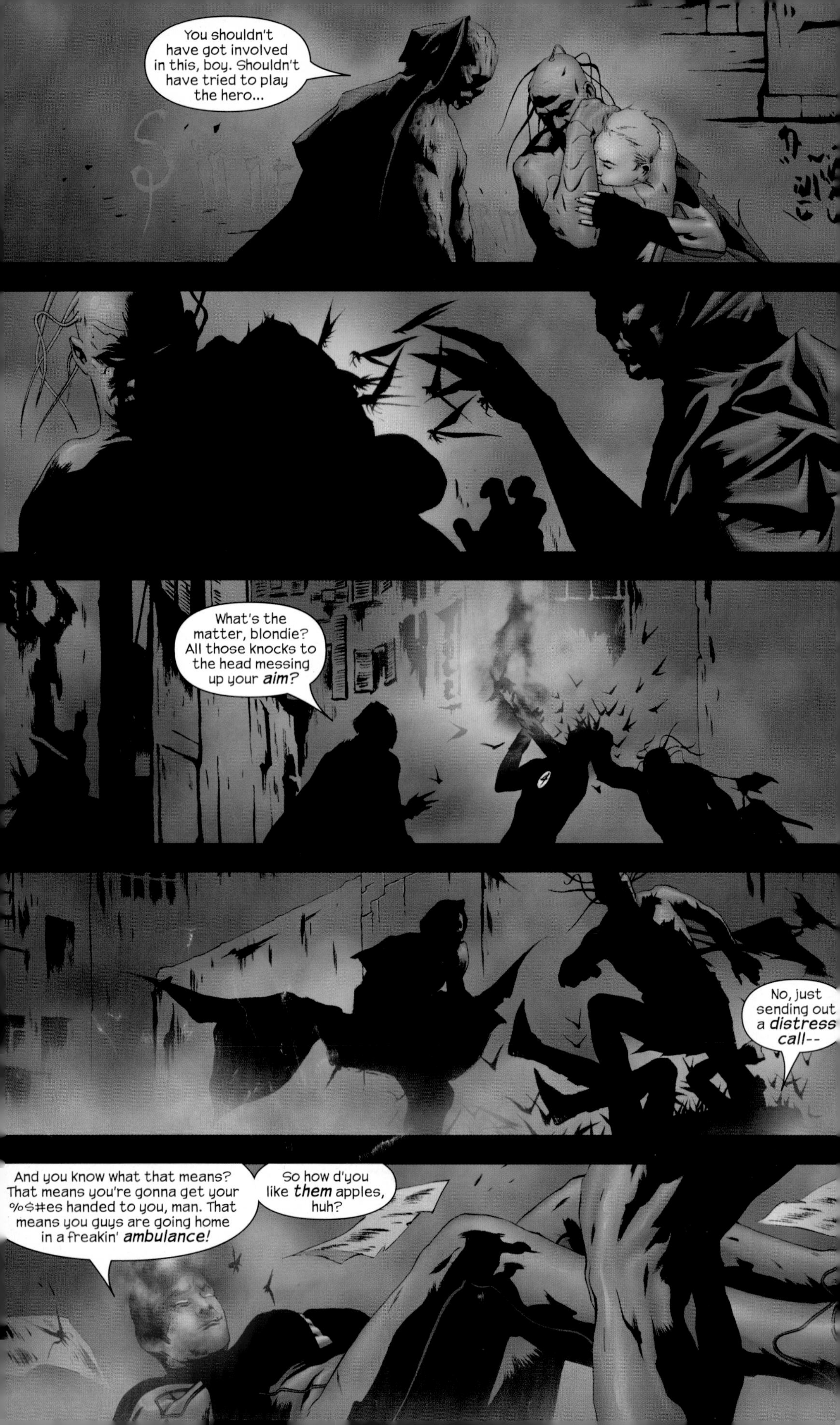
You shouldn't have got involved in this, boy. Shouldn't have tried to play the hero...
What's the matter, blondie? All those knocks to the head messing up your *aim*?
No, just sending out a *distress call*--
And you know what that means? That means you're gonna get your %$#es handed to you, man. That means you guys are going home in a freakin' *ambulance*!
So how d'you like *them* apples, huh?

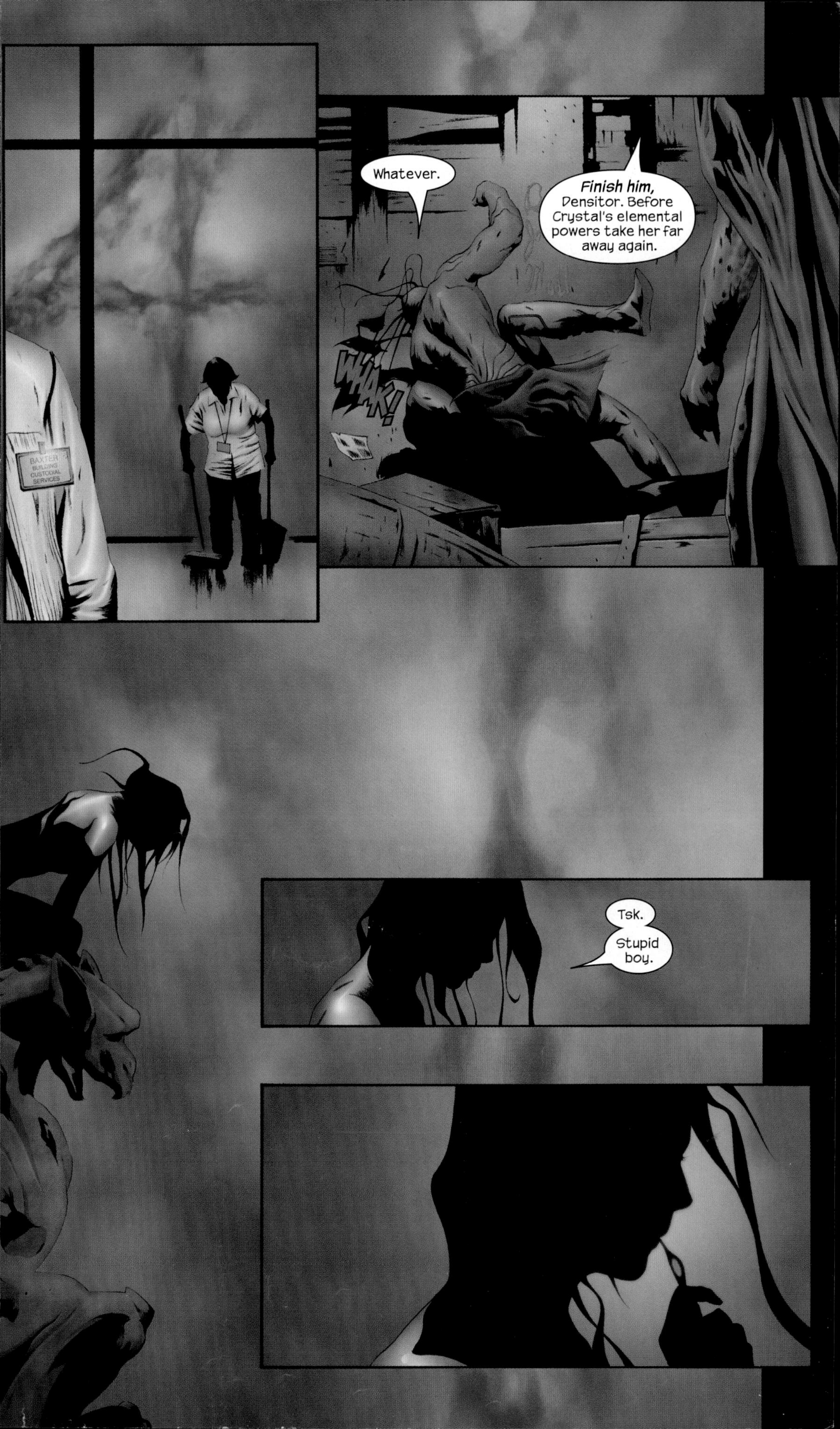
BAXTER BUILDING CUSTODIAL SERVICES
Whatever.
WHAK!
*Finish him,* Densitor. Before Crystal's elemental powers take her far away again.
Tsk.
Stupid boy.

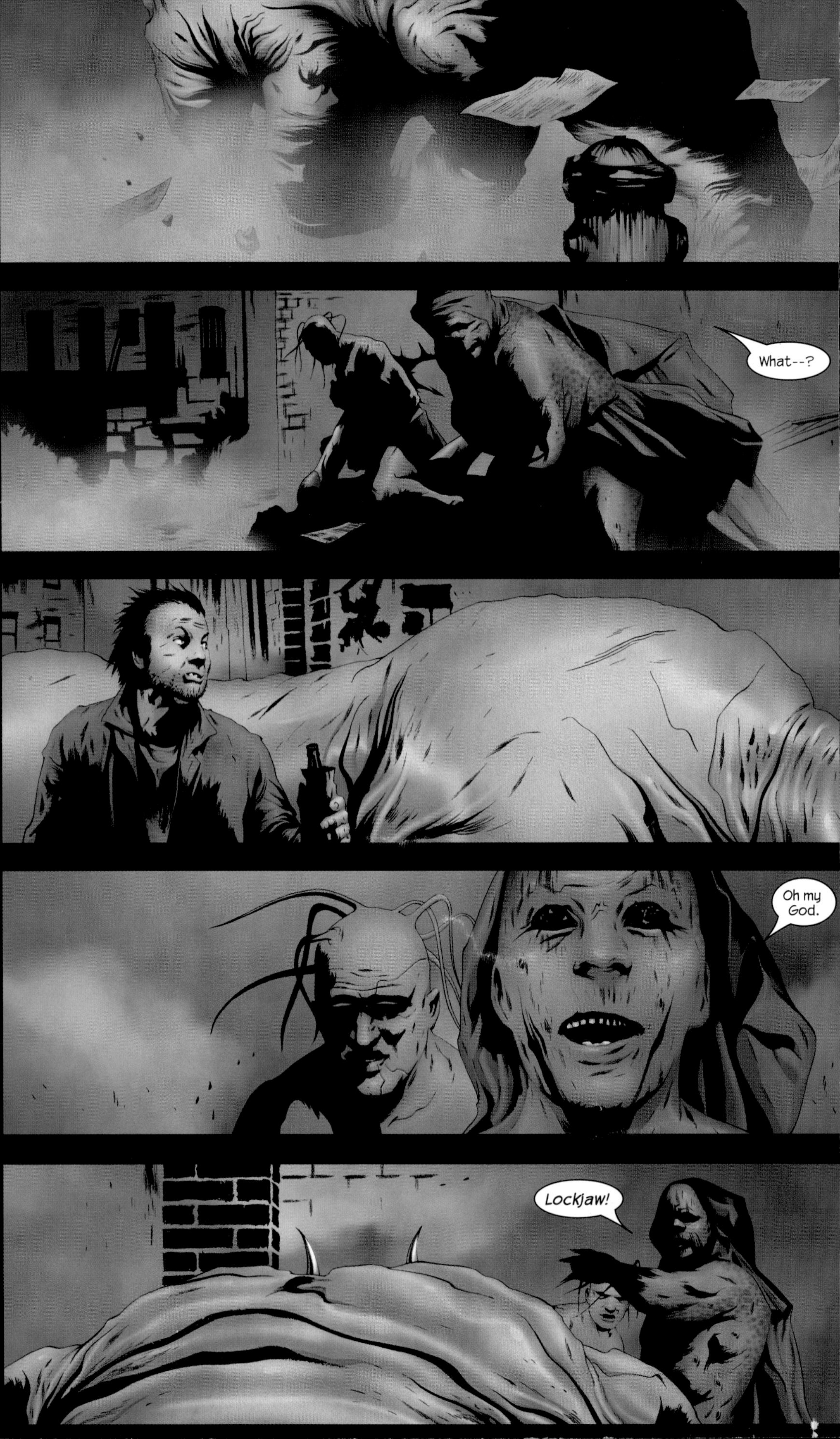
What--?
Oh my God.
Lockjaw!

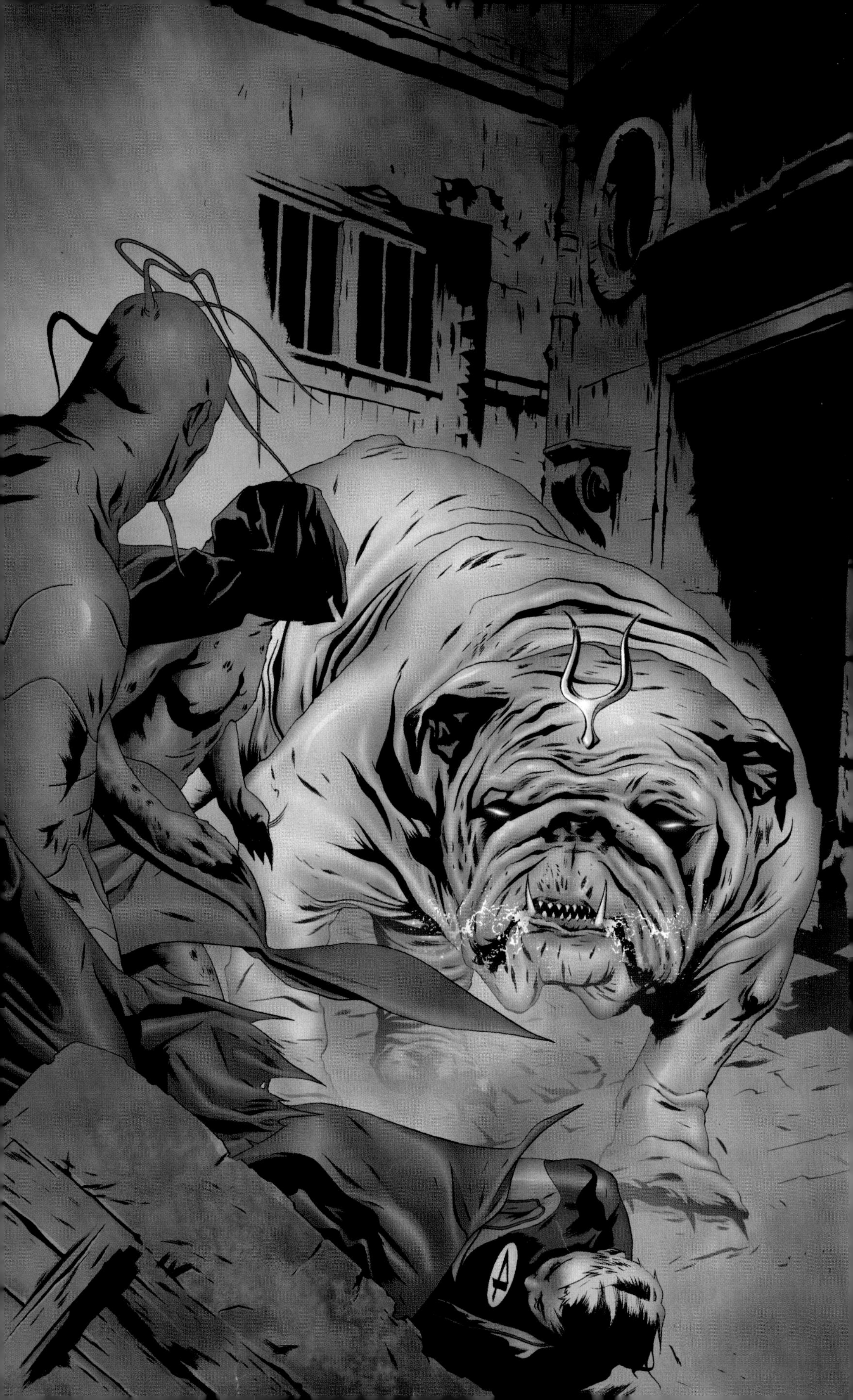

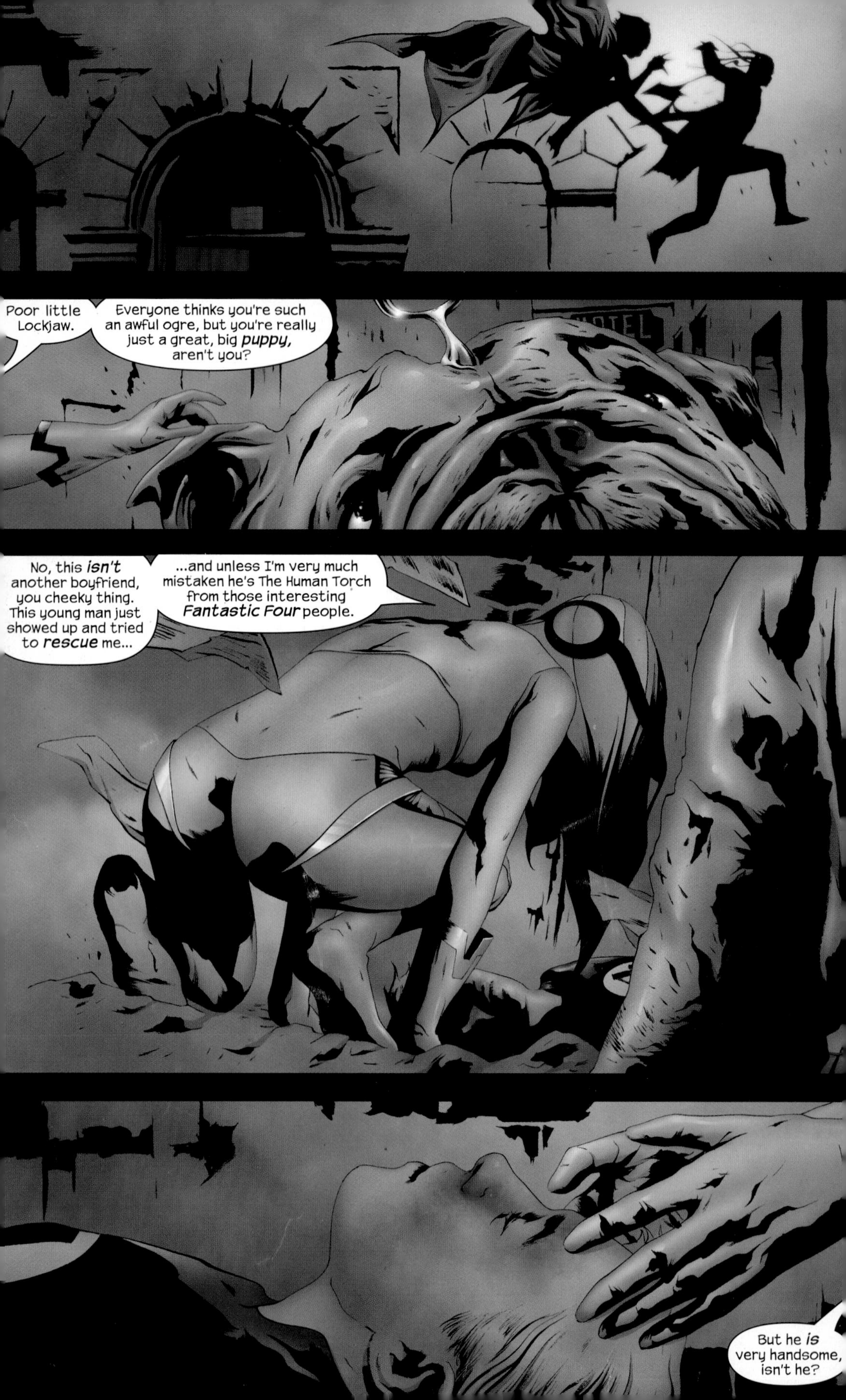
Poor little Lockjaw.
Everyone thinks you're such an awful ogre, but you're really just a great, big puppy, aren't you?
HOTEL
No, this isn't another boyfriend, you cheeky thing. This young man just showed up and tried to rescue me...
...and unless I'm very much mistaken he's The Human Torch from those interesting Fantastic Four people.
But he is very handsome, isn't he?

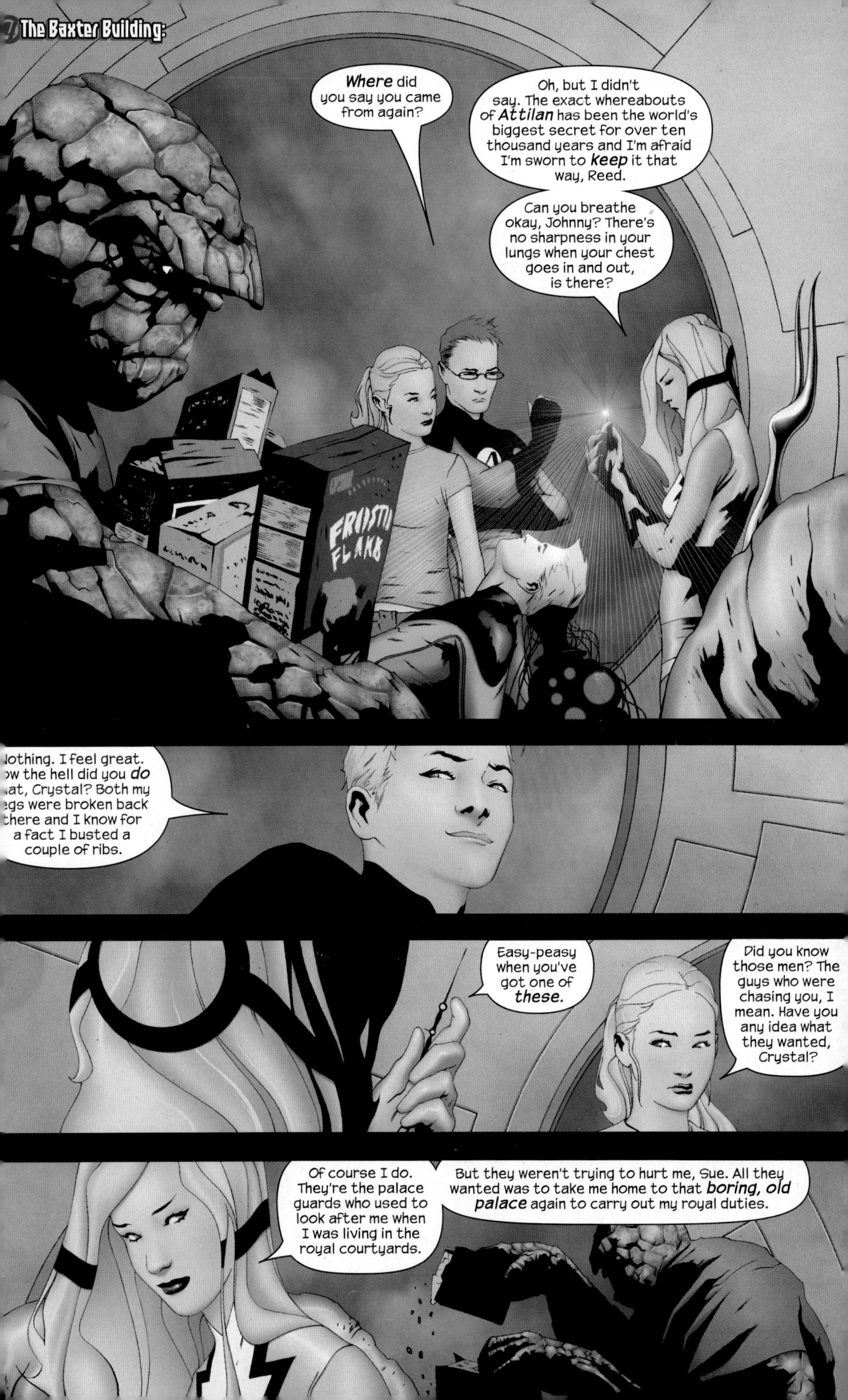
The Baxter Building:
Where did you say you came from again?
Oh, but I didn't say. The exact whereabouts of Attilan has been the world's biggest secret for over ten thousand years and I'm afraid I'm sworn to keep it that way, Reed.
Can you breathe okay, Johnny? There's no sharpness in your lungs when your chest goes in and out, is there?
FROSTIE FLAKES
lothing. I feel great. ow the hell did you do at, Crystal? Both my gs were broken back there and I know for a fact I busted a couple of ribs.
Easy-peasy when you've got one of these.
Did you know those men? The guys who were chasing you, I mean. Have you any idea what they wanted, Crystal?
Of course I do. They're the palace guards who used to look after me when I was living in the royal courtyards.
But they weren't trying to hurt me, Sue. All they wanted was to take me home to that boring, old palace again to carry out my royal duties.

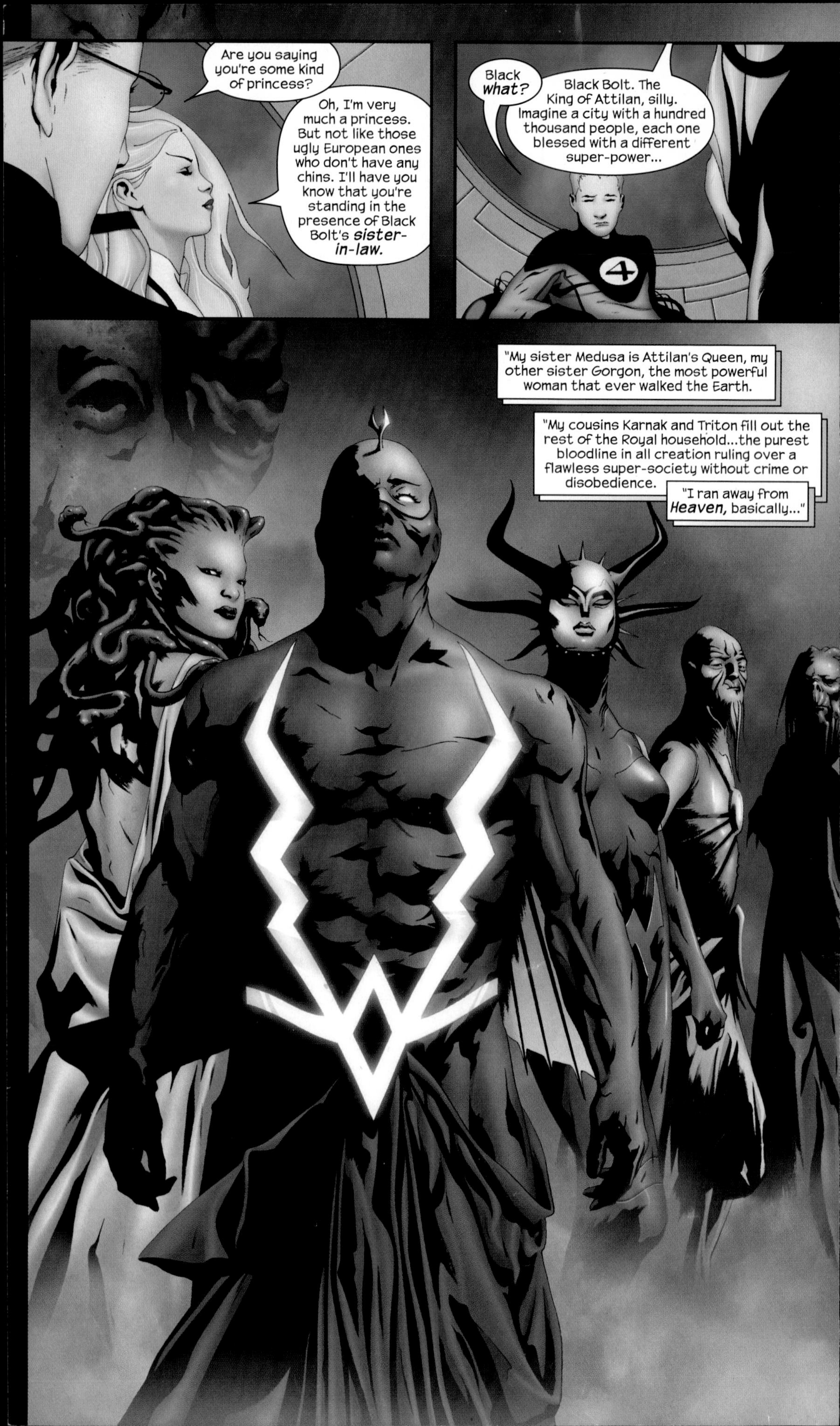
Are you saying you're some kind of princess?
Oh, I'm very much a princess. But not like those ugly European ones who don't have any chins. I'll have you know that you're standing in the presence of Black Bolt's sister-in-law.
Black what?
Black Bolt. The King of Attilan, silly. Imagine a city with a hundred thousand people, each one blessed with a different super-power...
"My sister Medusa is Attilan's Queen, my other sister Gorgon, the most powerful woman that ever walked the Earth.
"My cousins Karnak and Triton fill out the rest of the Royal household...the purest bloodline in all creation ruling over a flawless super-society without crime or disobedience.
"I ran away from Heaven, basically..."

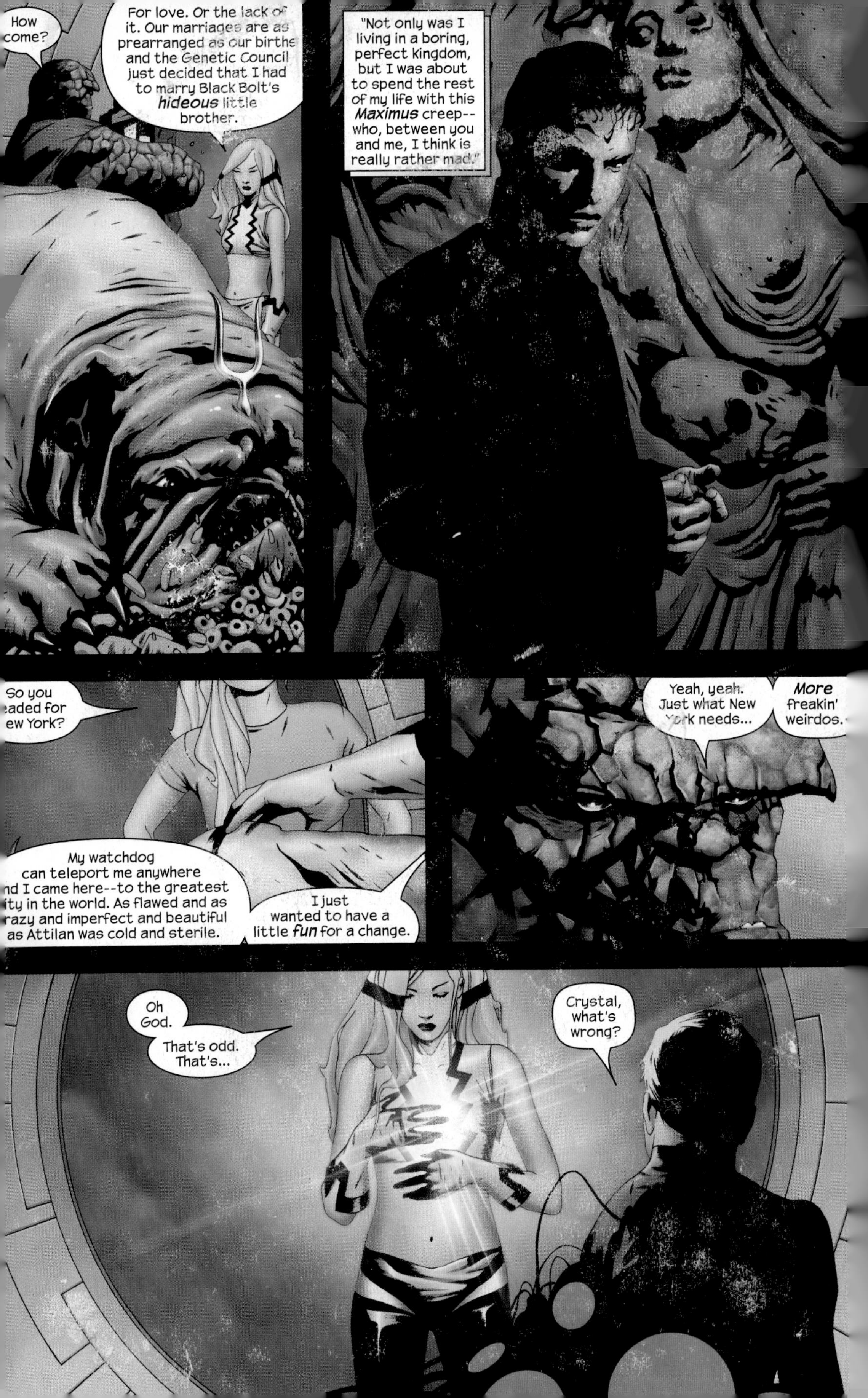
How come?
For love. Or the lack of it. Our marriages are as prearranged as our births and the Genetic Council just decided that I had to marry Black Bolt's *hideous* little brother.
"Not only was I living in a boring, perfect kingdom, but I was about to spend the rest of my life with this *Maximus* creep--who, between you and me, I think is really rather mad."
So you eaded for ew York?
My watchdog can teleport me anywhere nd I came here--to the greatest ity in the world. As flawed and as razy and imperfect and beautiful as Attilan was cold and sterile.
I just wanted to have a little *fun* for a change.
Yeah, yeah. Just what New York needs...
*More* freakin' weirdos.
Oh God.
That's odd. That's...
Crystal, what's wrong?

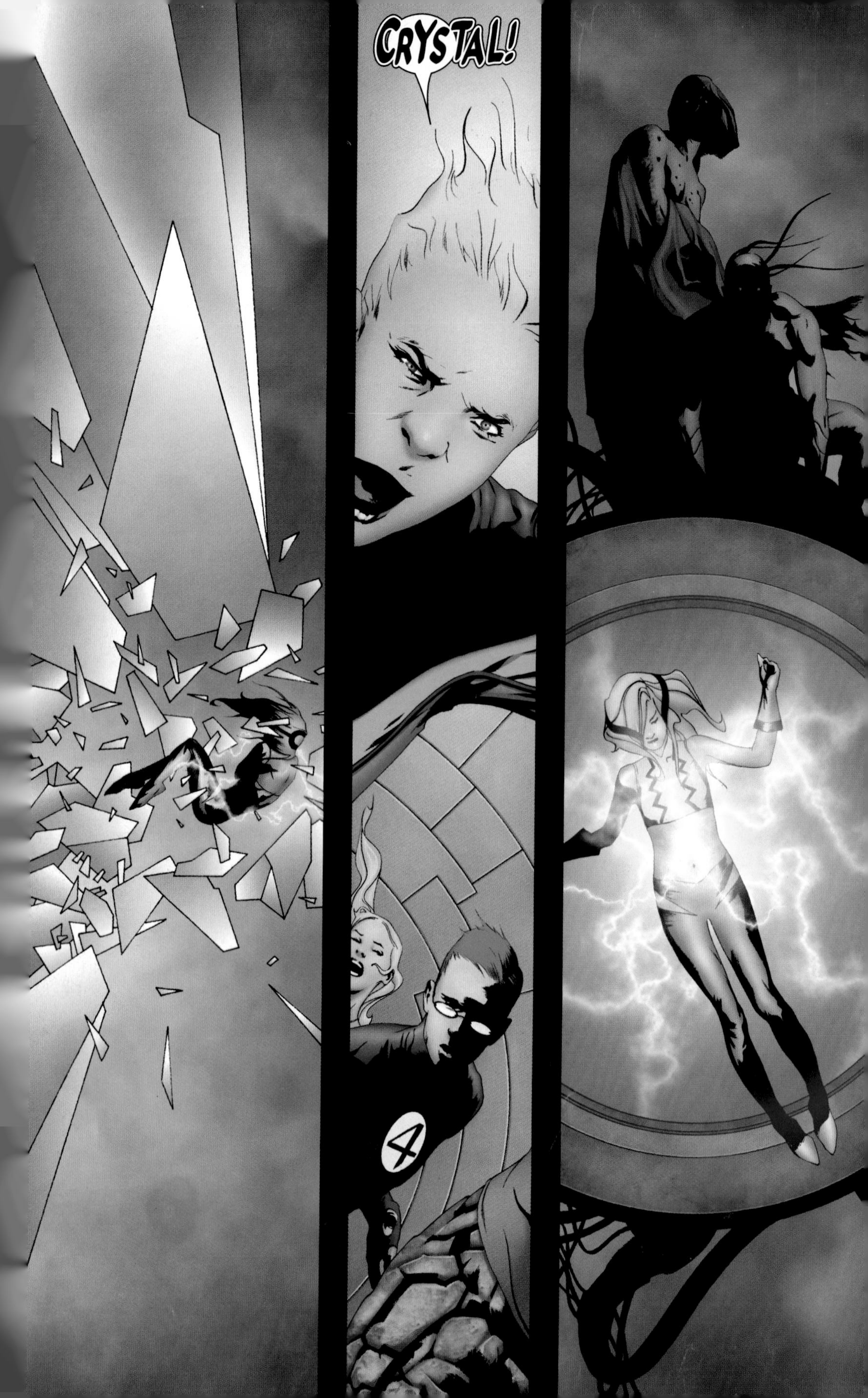
CRYSTAL!

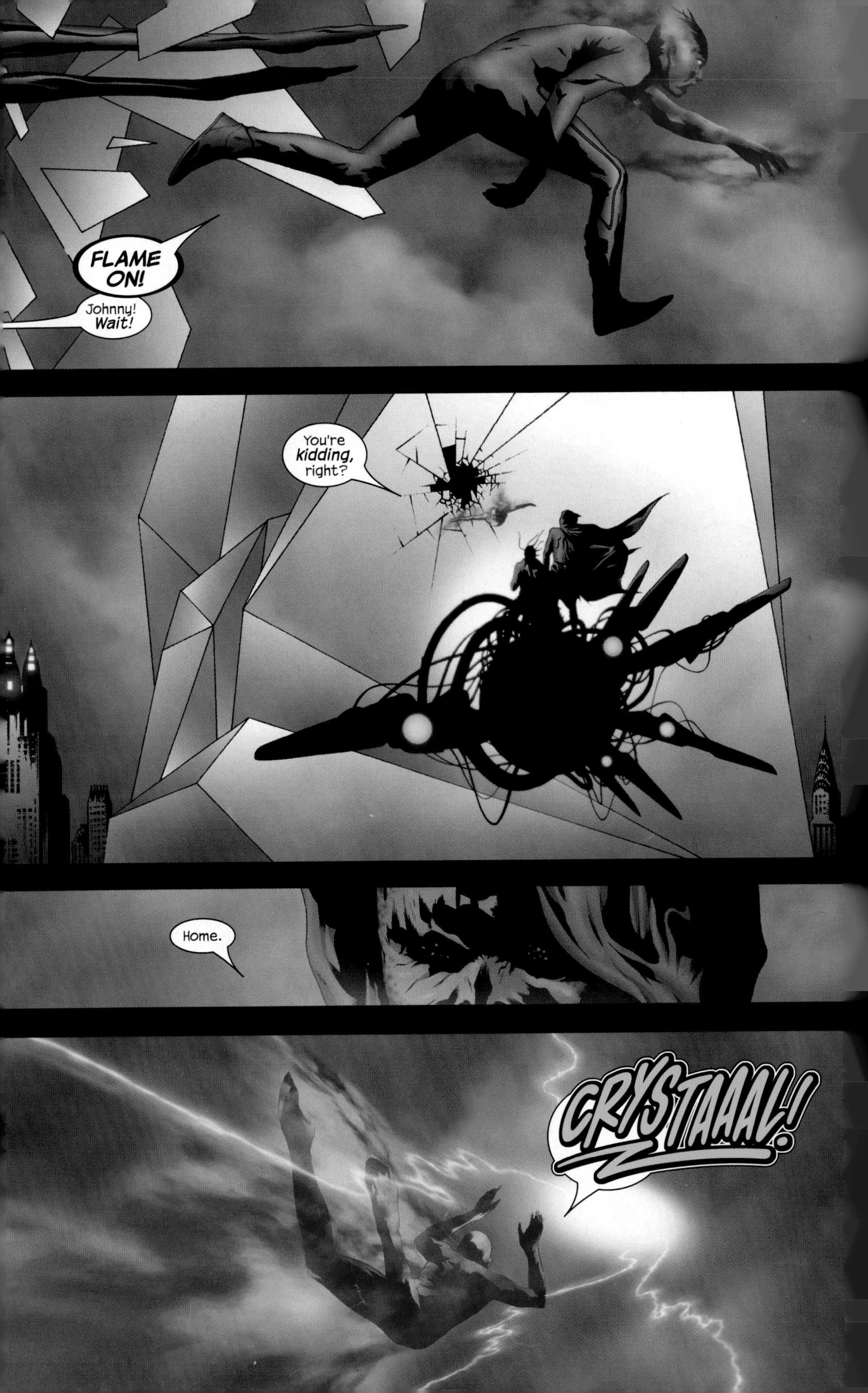
FLAME ON!
Johnny! Wait!
You're kidding, right?
Home.
CRYSTAAAL!

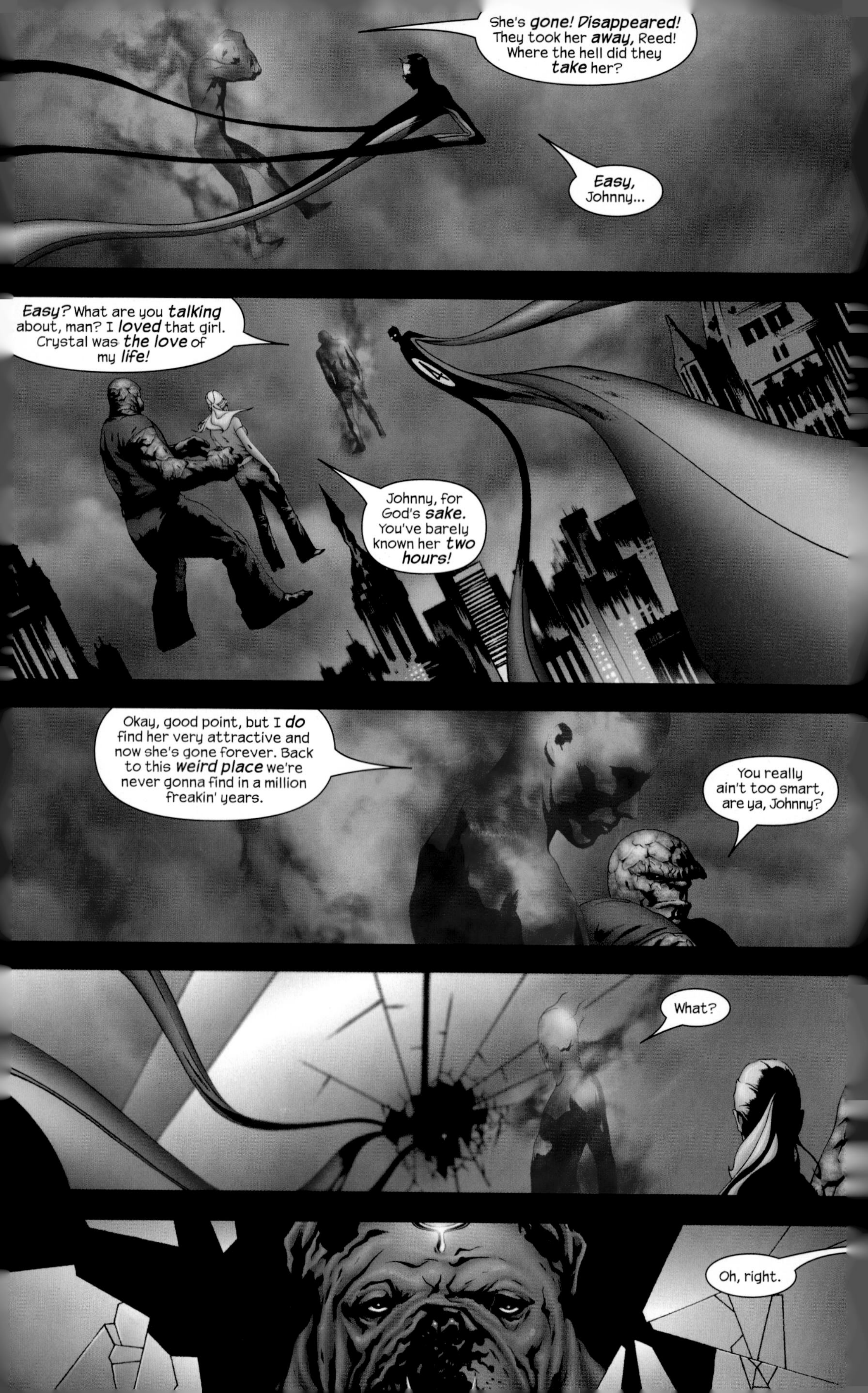
She's gone! Disappeared! They took her away, Reed! Where the hell did they take her?
Easy, Johnny...
Easy? What are you talking about, man? I loved that girl. Crystal was the love of my life!
Johnny, for God's sake. You've barely known her two hours!
Okay, good point, but I do find her very attractive and now she's gone forever. Back to this weird place we're never gonna find in a million freakin' years.
You really ain't too smart, are ya, Johnny?
What?
Oh, right.

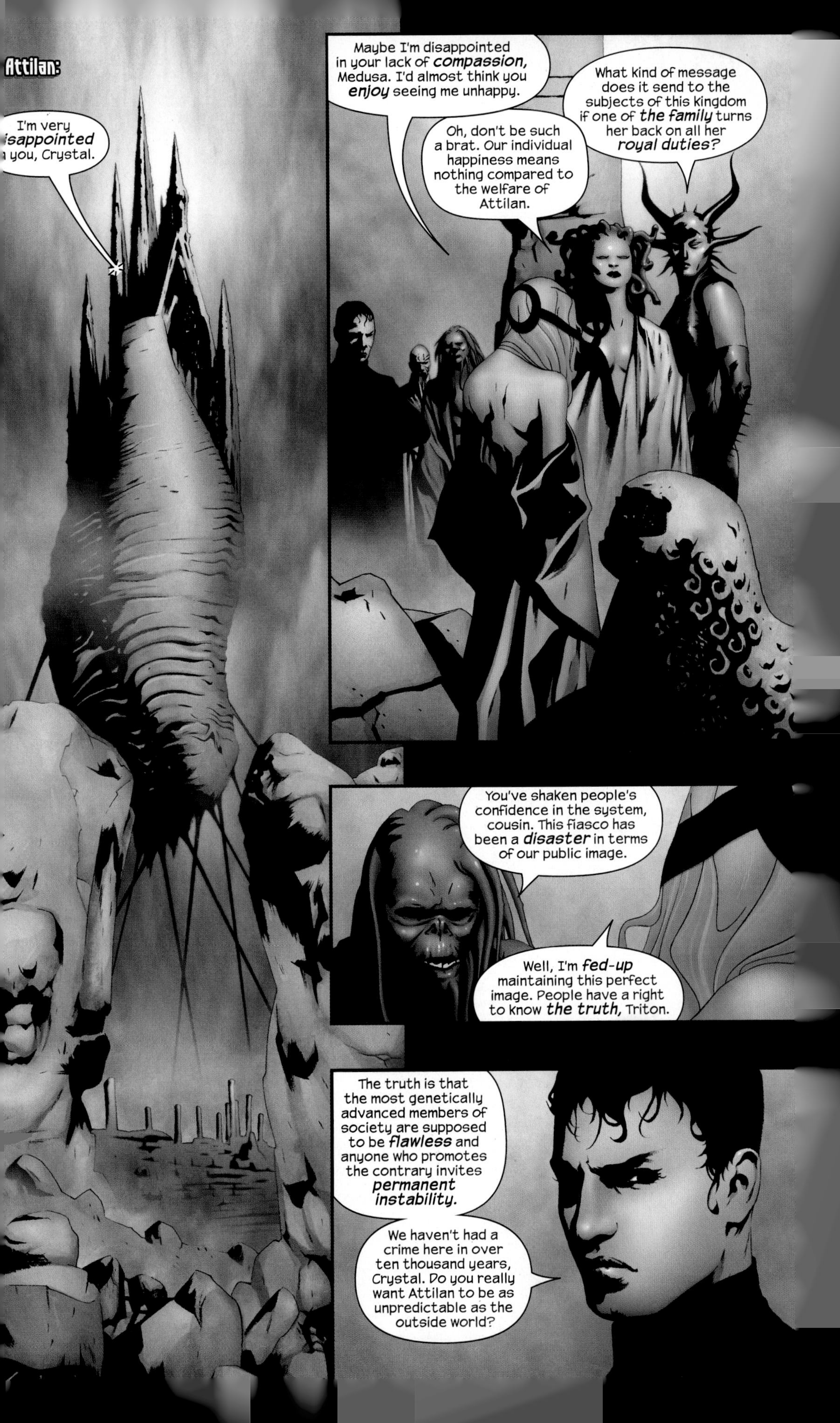
Attilan:
I'm very isappointed n you, Crystal.
Maybe I'm disappointed in your lack of compassion, Medusa. I'd almost think you enjoy seeing me unhappy.
Oh, don't be such a brat. Our individual happiness means nothing compared to the welfare of Attilan.
What kind of message does it send to the subjects of this kingdom if one of the family turns her back on all her royal duties?
You've shaken people's confidence in the system, cousin. This fiasco has been a disaster in terms of our public image.
Well, I'm fed-up maintaining this perfect image. People have a right to know the truth, Triton.
The truth is that the most genetically advanced members of society are supposed to be flawless and anyone who promotes the contrary invites permanent instability.
We haven't had a crime here in over ten thousand years, Crystal. Do you really want Attilan to be as unpredictable as the outside world?

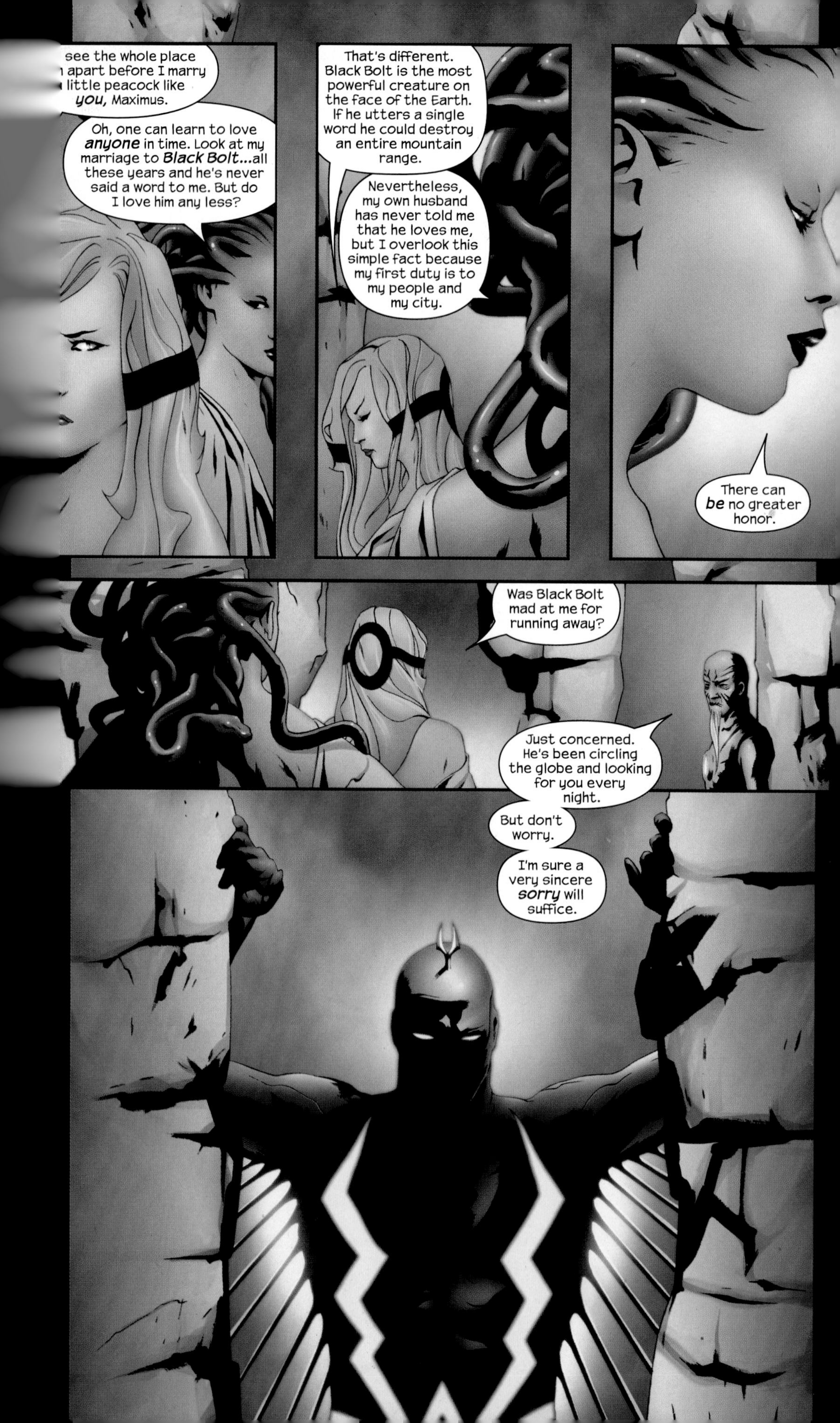
see the whole place
apart before I marry
little peacock like
*you,* Maximus.
Oh, one can learn to love *anyone* in time. Look at my marriage to *Black Bolt...*all these years and he's never said a word to me. But do I love him any less?
That's different. Black Bolt is the most powerful creature on the face of the Earth. If he utters a single word he could destroy an entire mountain range.
Nevertheless, my own husband has never told me that he loves me, but I overlook this simple fact because my first duty is to my people and my city.
There can *be* no greater honor.
Was Black Bolt mad at me for running away?
Just concerned. He's been circling the globe and looking for you every night.
But don't worry.
I'm sure a very sincere *sorry* will suffice.

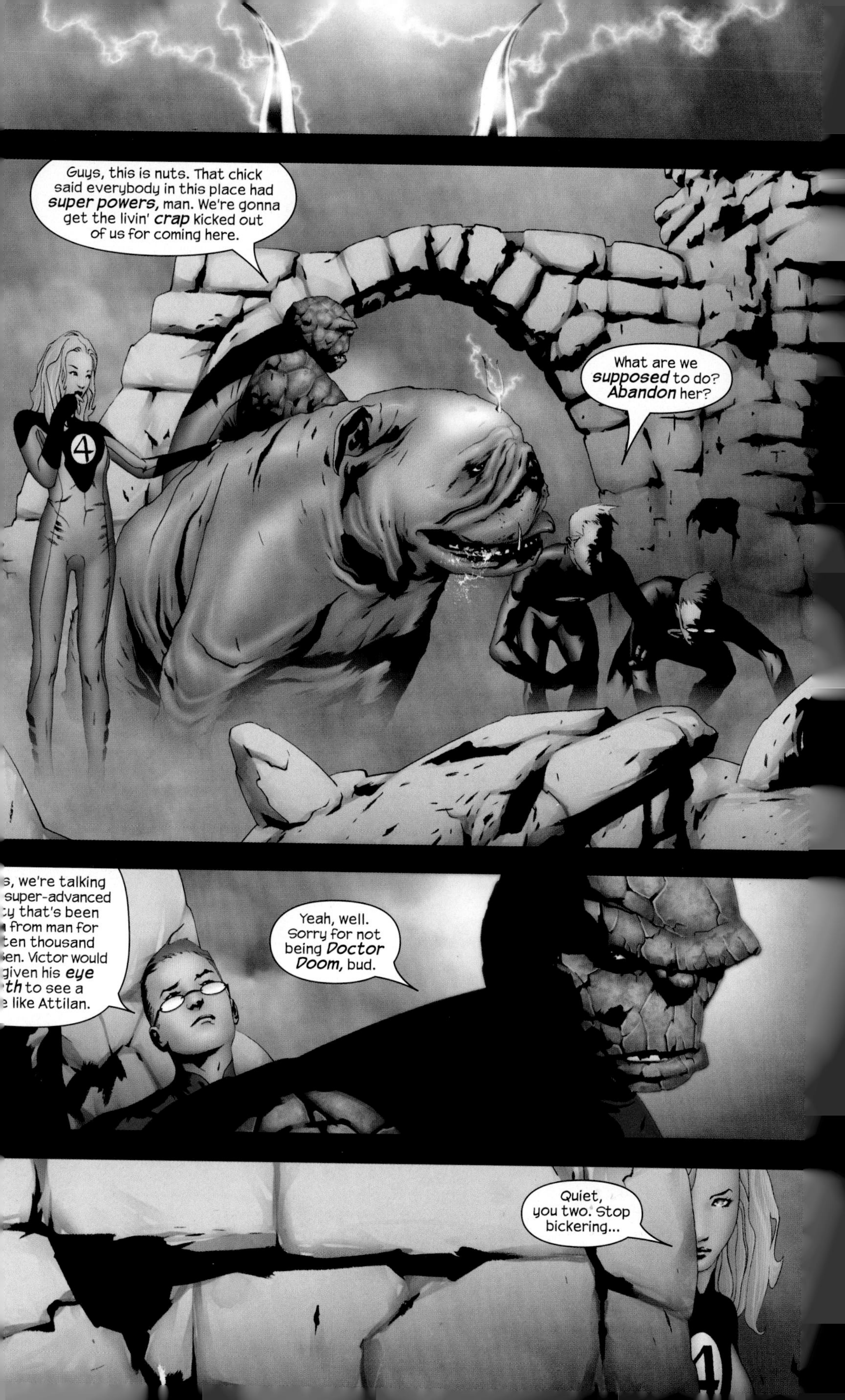
Guys, this is nuts. That chick said everybody in this place had super powers, man. We're gonna get the livin' crap kicked out of us for coming here.
What are we supposed to do? Abandon her?
s, we're talking super-advanced cy that's been from man for ten thousand en. Victor would given his eye th to see a e like Attilan.
Yeah, well. Sorry for not being Doctor Doom, bud.
Quiet, you two. Stop bickering...

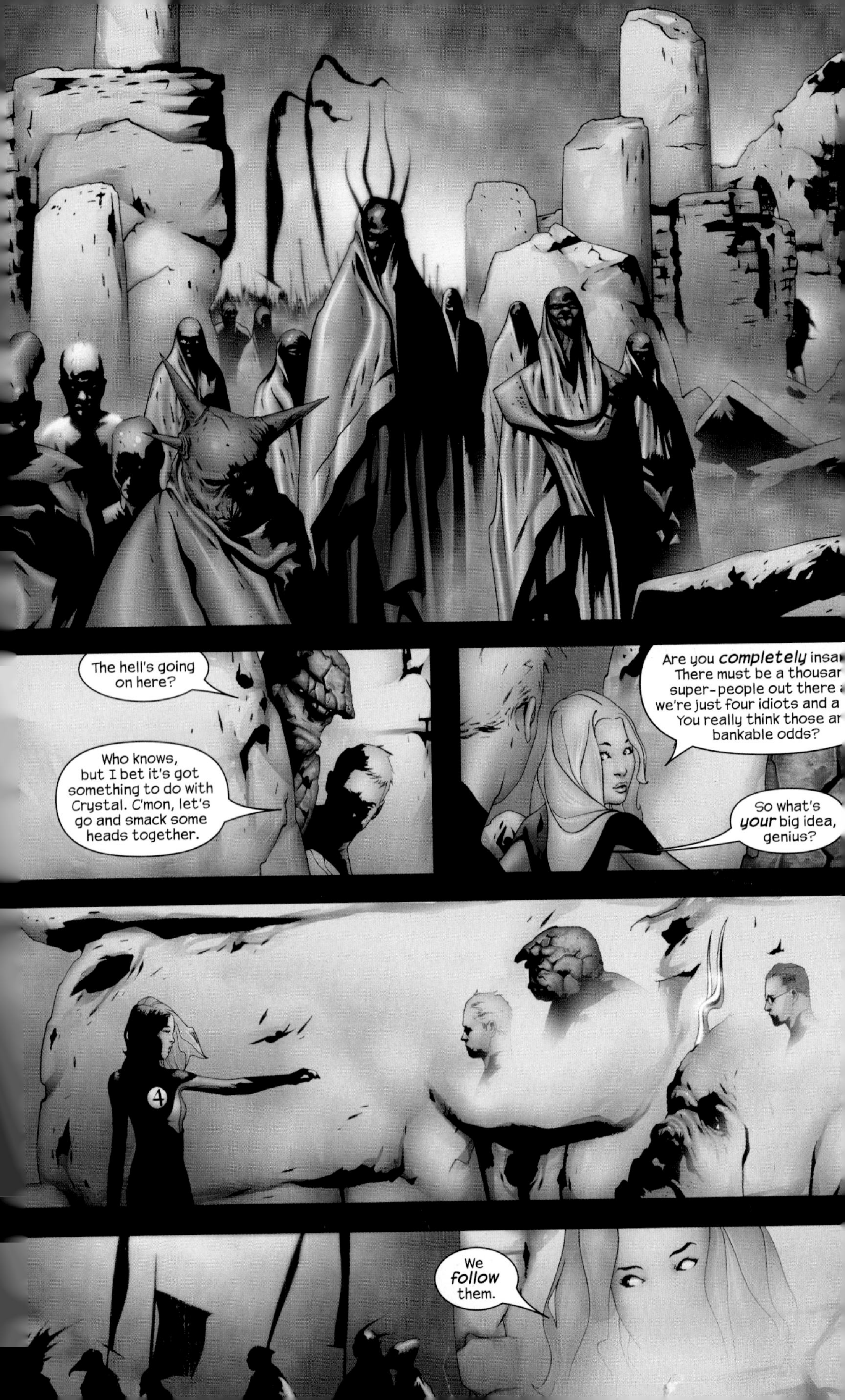
The hell's going on here?
Who knows, but I bet it's got something to do with Crystal. C'mon, let's go and smack some heads together.
Are you *completely* insa
There must be a thousar
super-people out there
we're just four idiots and a
You really think those ar
bankable odds?
So what's *your* big idea, genius?
We *follow* them.

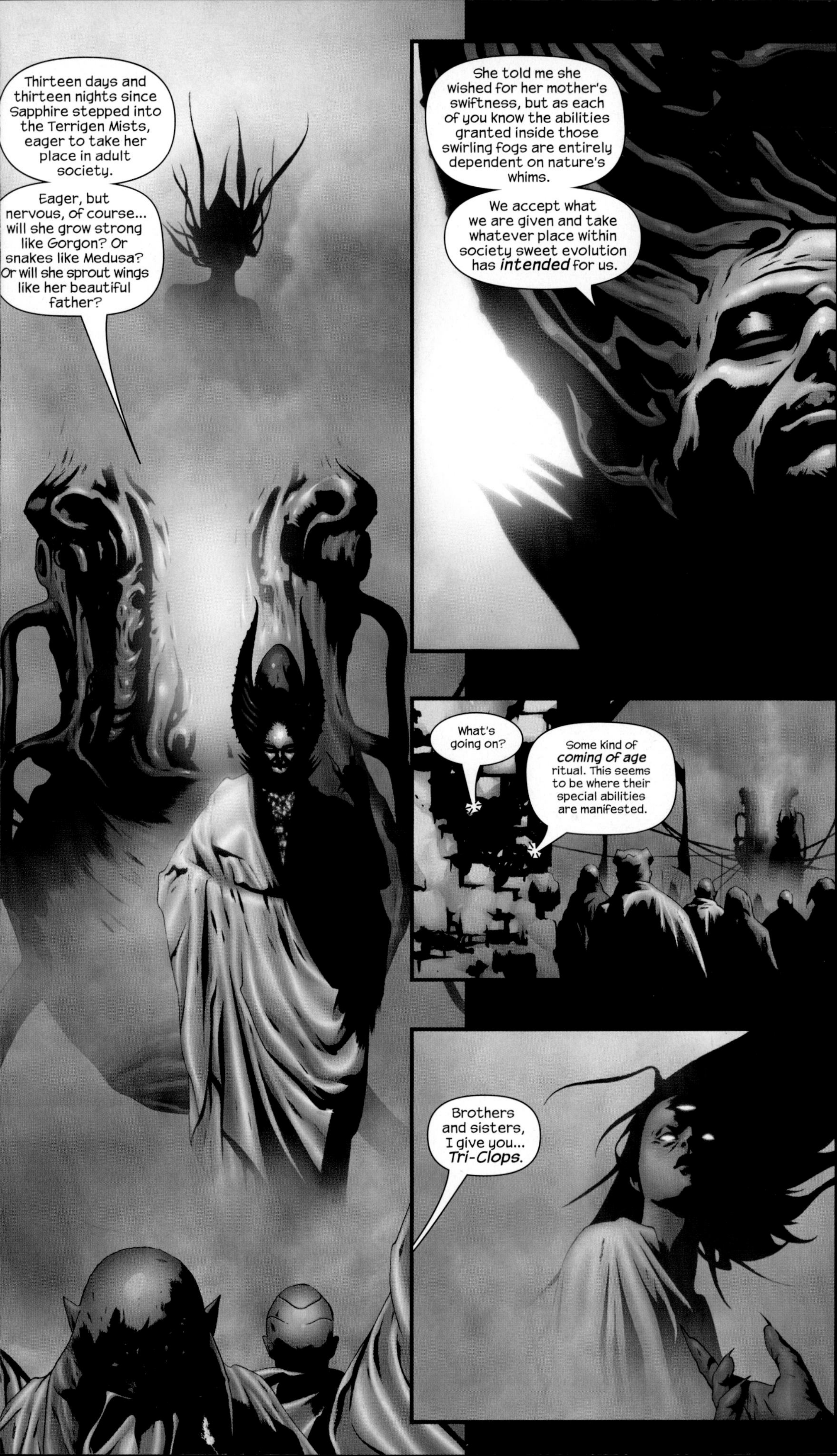
Thirteen days and thirteen nights since Sapphire stepped into the Terrigen Mists, eager to take her place in adult society.
Eager, but nervous, of course... will she grow strong like Gorgon? Or snakes like Medusa? Or will she sprout wings like her beautiful father?
She told me she wished for her mother's swiftness, but as each of you know the abilities granted inside those swirling fogs are entirely dependent on nature's whims.
We accept what we are given and take whatever place within society sweet evolution has *intended* for us.
What's going on?
Some kind of *coming of age* ritual. This seems to be where their special abilities are manifested.
Brothers and sisters, I give you... *Tri-Clops*.

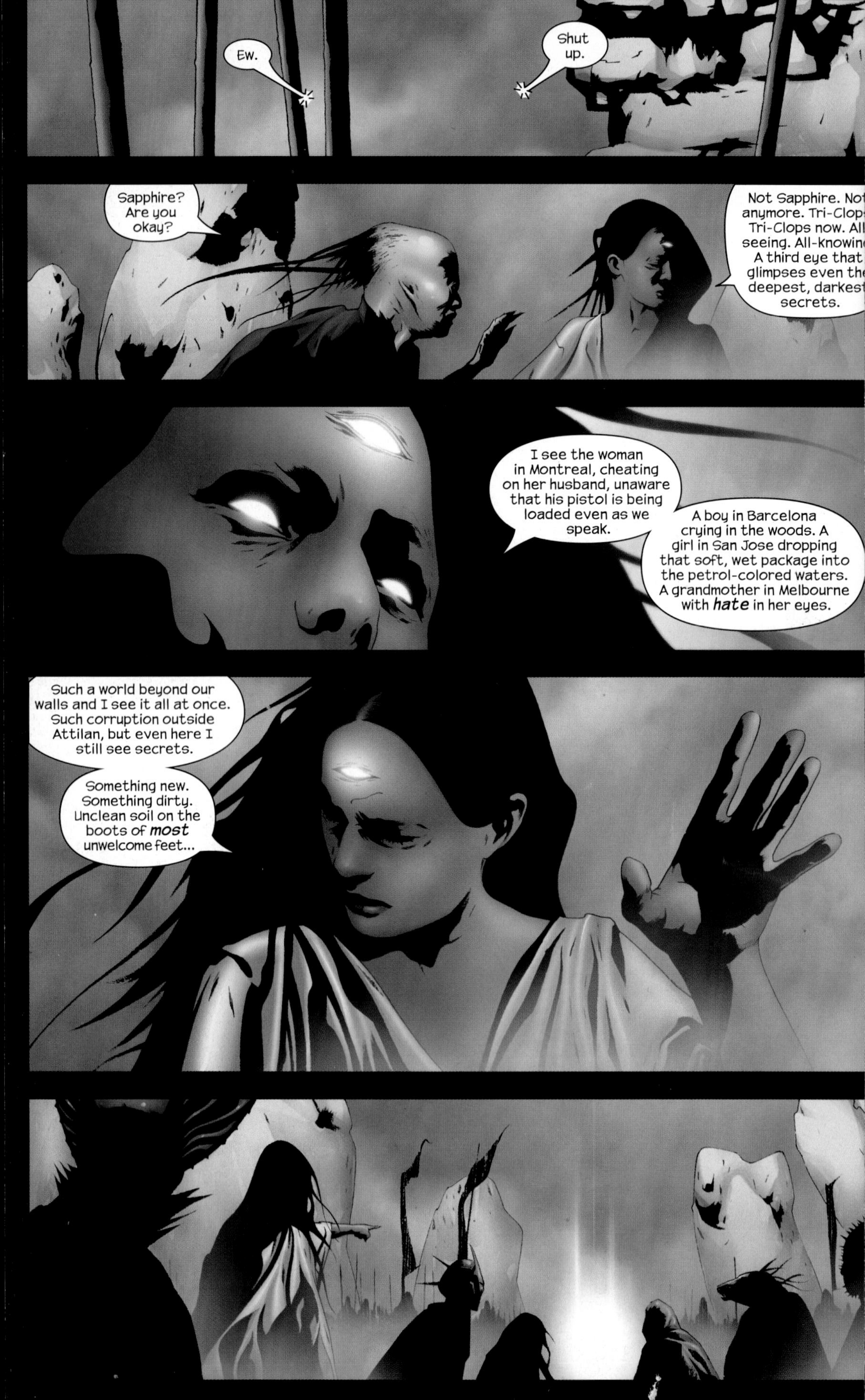

Ew.
Shut up.
Sapphire? Are you okay?
Not Sapphire. Not anymore. Tri-Clops. Tri-Clops now. All seeing. All-knowing. A third eye that glimpses even the deepest, darkest secrets.
I see the woman in Montreal, cheating on her husband, unaware that his pistol is being loaded even as we speak.
A boy in Barcelona crying in the woods. A girl in San Jose dropping that soft, wet package into the petrol-colored waters. A grandmother in Melbourne with *hate* in her eyes.
Such a world beyond our walls and I see it all at once. Such corruption outside Attilan, but even here I still see secrets.
Something new. Something dirty. Unclean soil on the boots of *most* unwelcome feet...

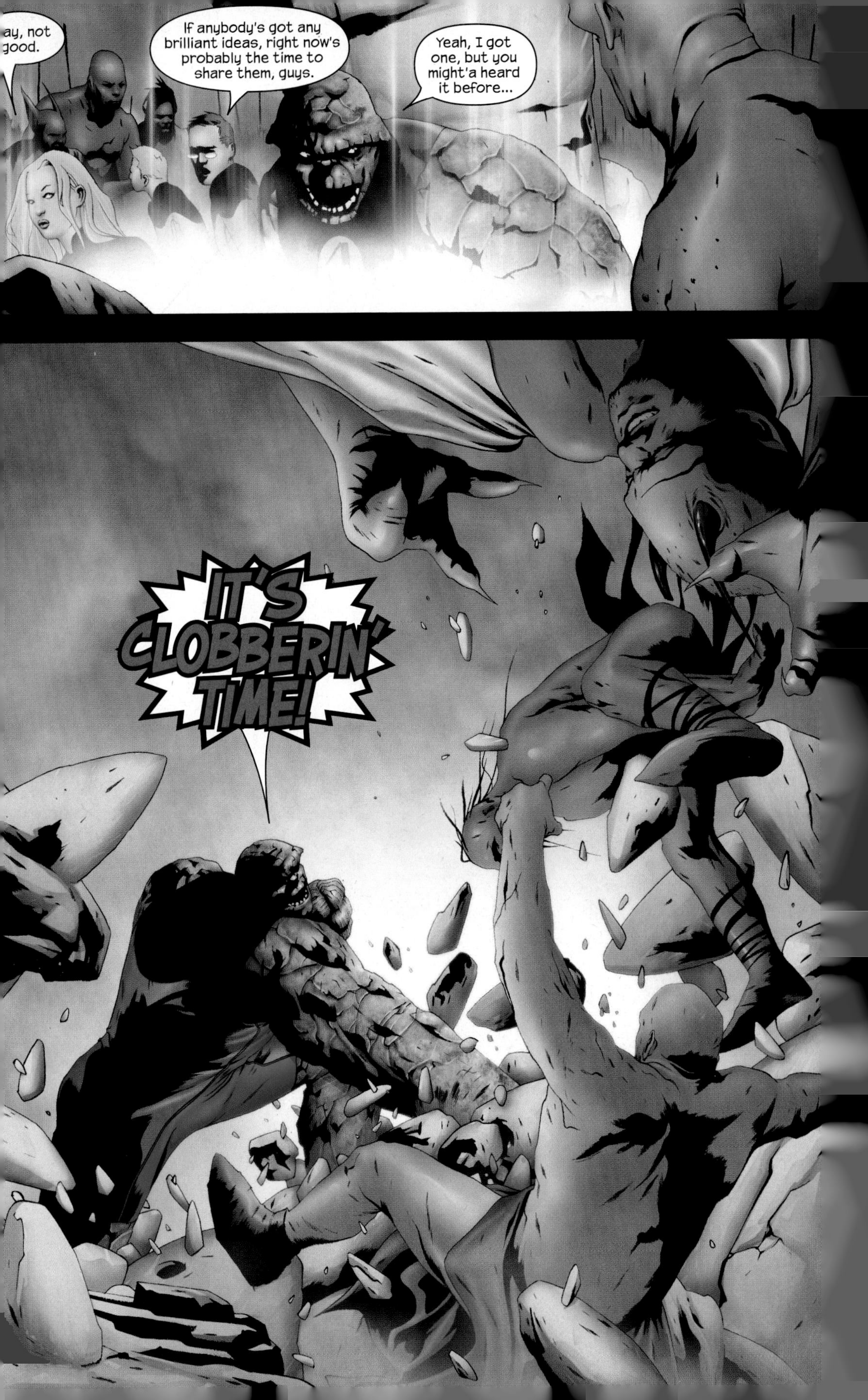
ay, not
good.
If anybody's got any brilliant ideas, right now's probably the time to share them, guys.
Yeah, I got one, but you might'a heard it before...
IT'S CLOBBERIN' TIME!

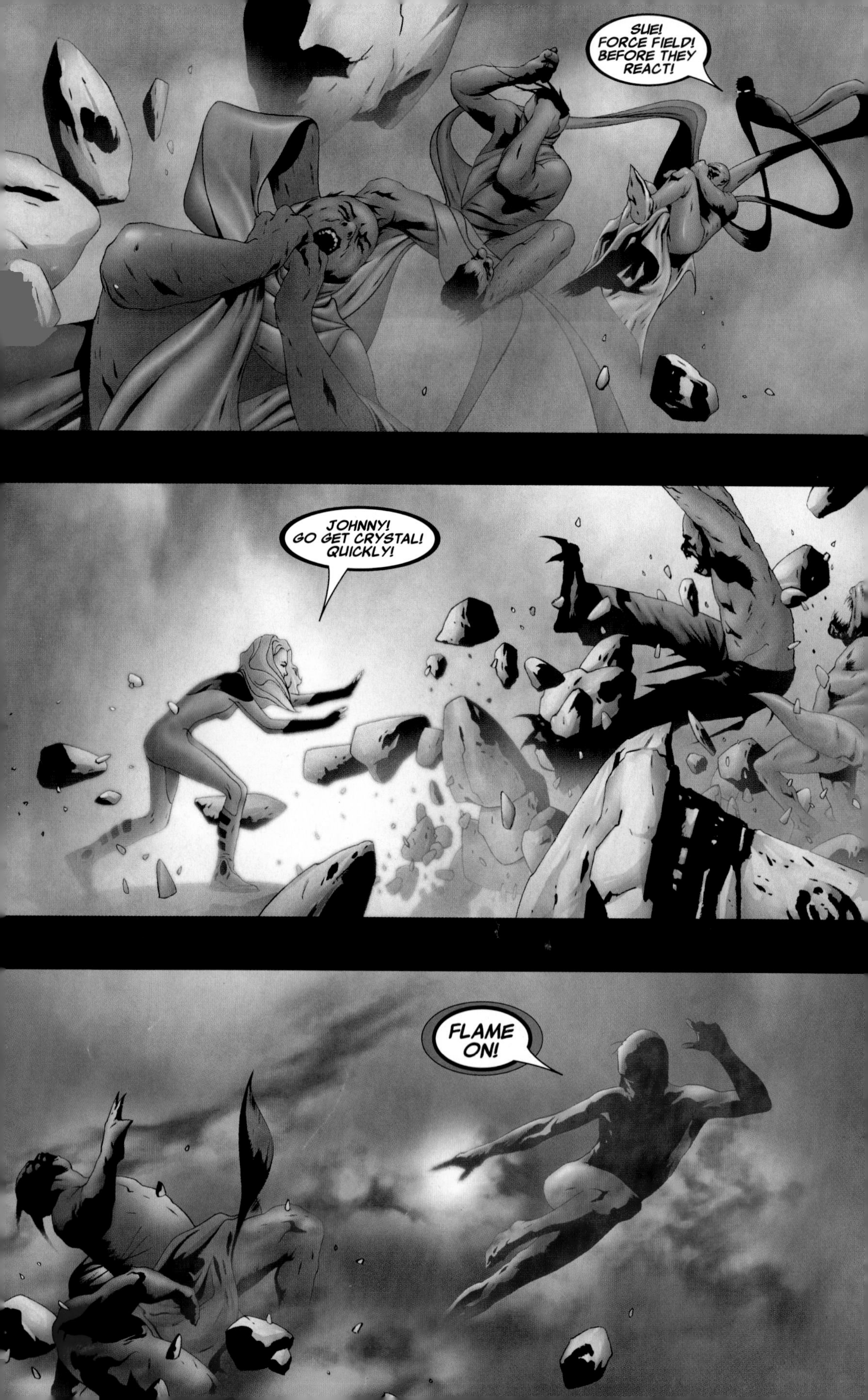
SUE! FORCE FIELD! BEFORE THEY REACT!
JOHNNY! GO GET CRYSTAL! QUICKLY!
FLAME ON!

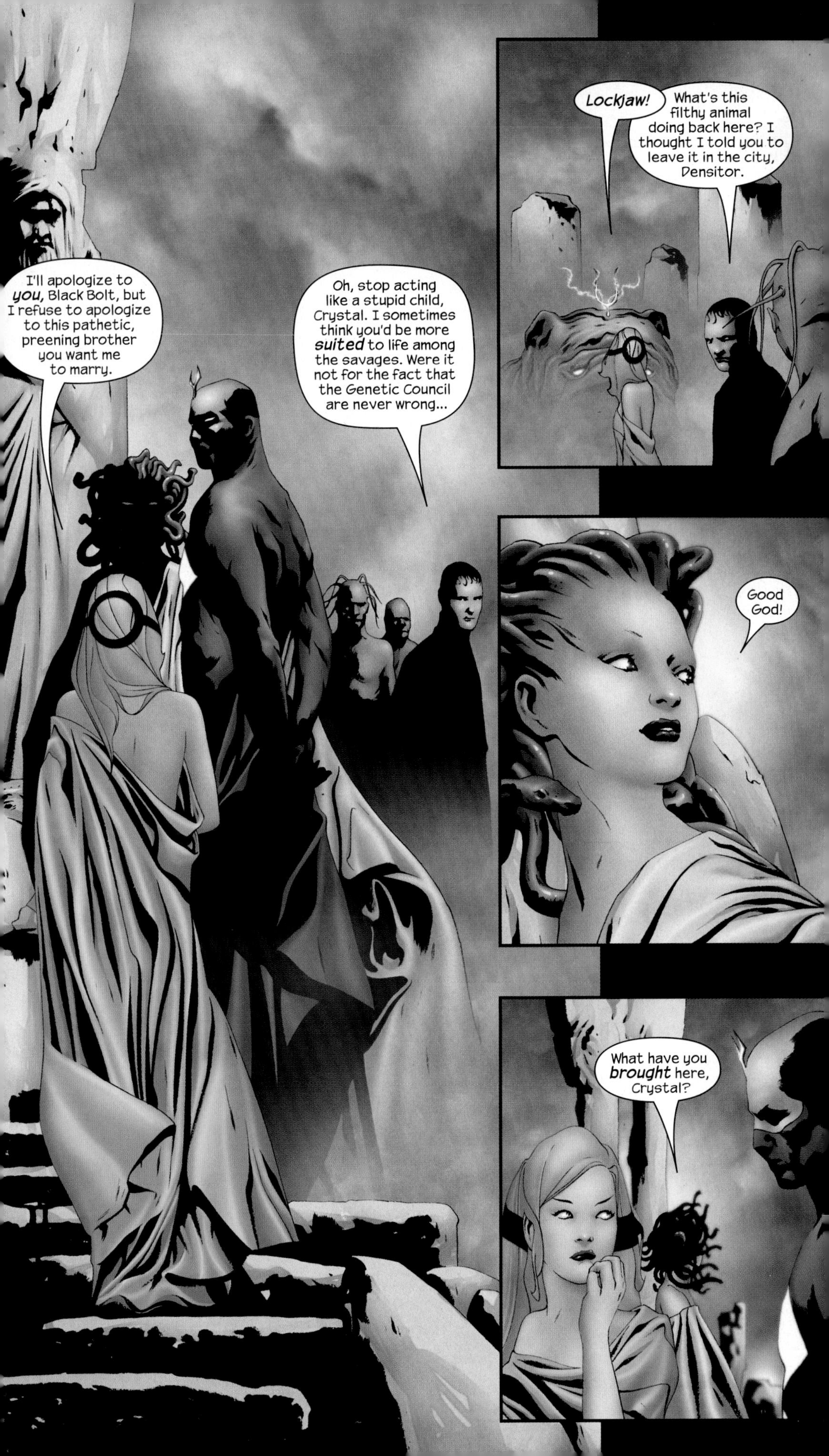
I'll apologize to *you,* Black Bolt, but I refuse to apologize to this pathetic, preening brother you want me to marry.
Oh, stop acting like a stupid child, Crystal. I sometimes think you'd be more *suited* to life among the savages. Were it not for the fact that the Genetic Council are never wrong...
*Lockjaw!*
What's this filthy animal doing back here? I thought I told you to leave it in the city, Densitor.
Good God!
What have you *brought* here, Crystal?

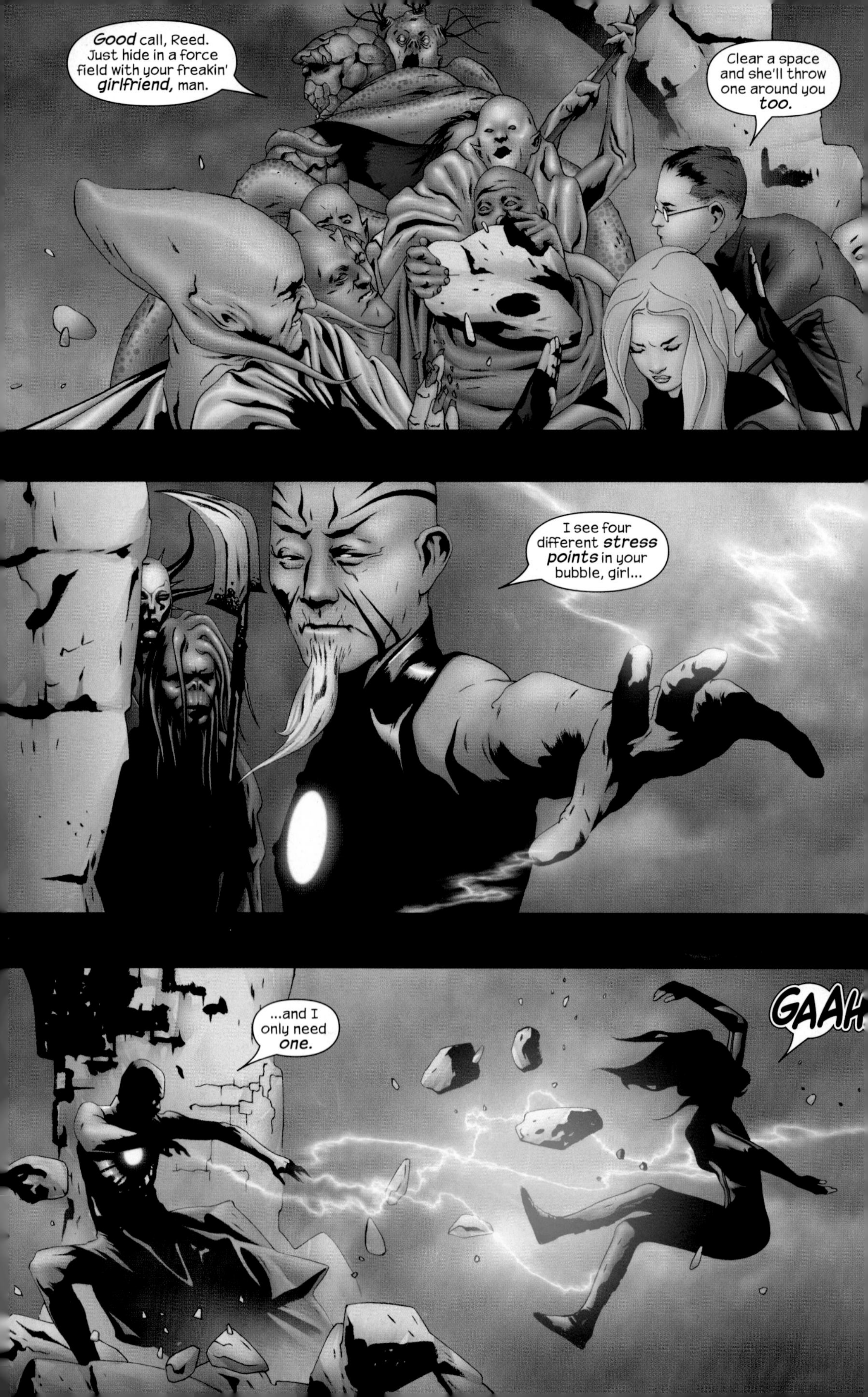
Good call, Reed. Just hide in a force field with your freakin' girlfriend, man.
Clear a space and she'll throw one around you too.
I see four different stress points in your bubble, girl...
...and I only need one.
GAAH

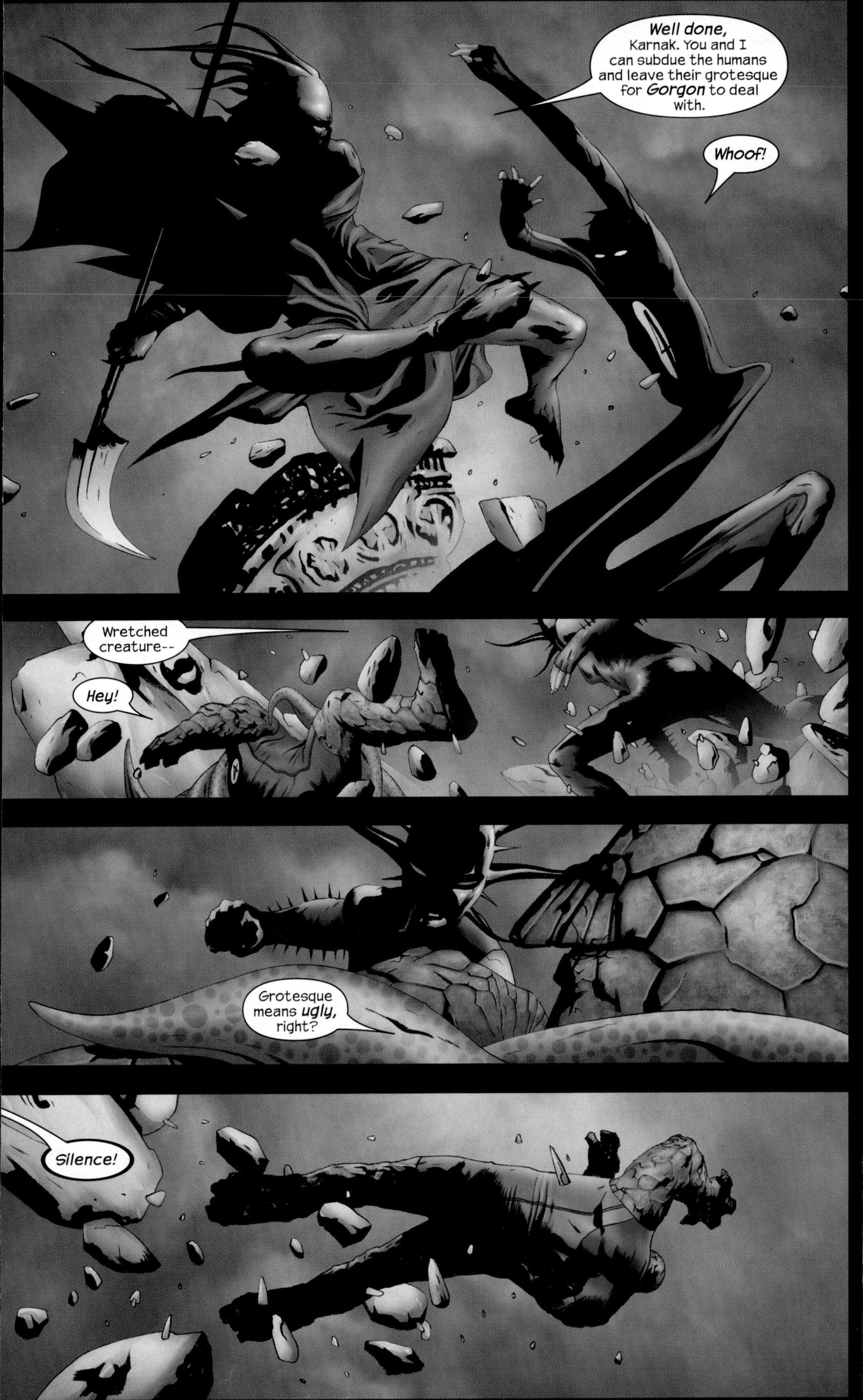
Well done, Karnak. You and I can subdue the humans and leave their grotesque for Gorgon to deal with.
Whoof!
Wretched creature--
Hey!
Grotesque means ugly, right?
Silence!

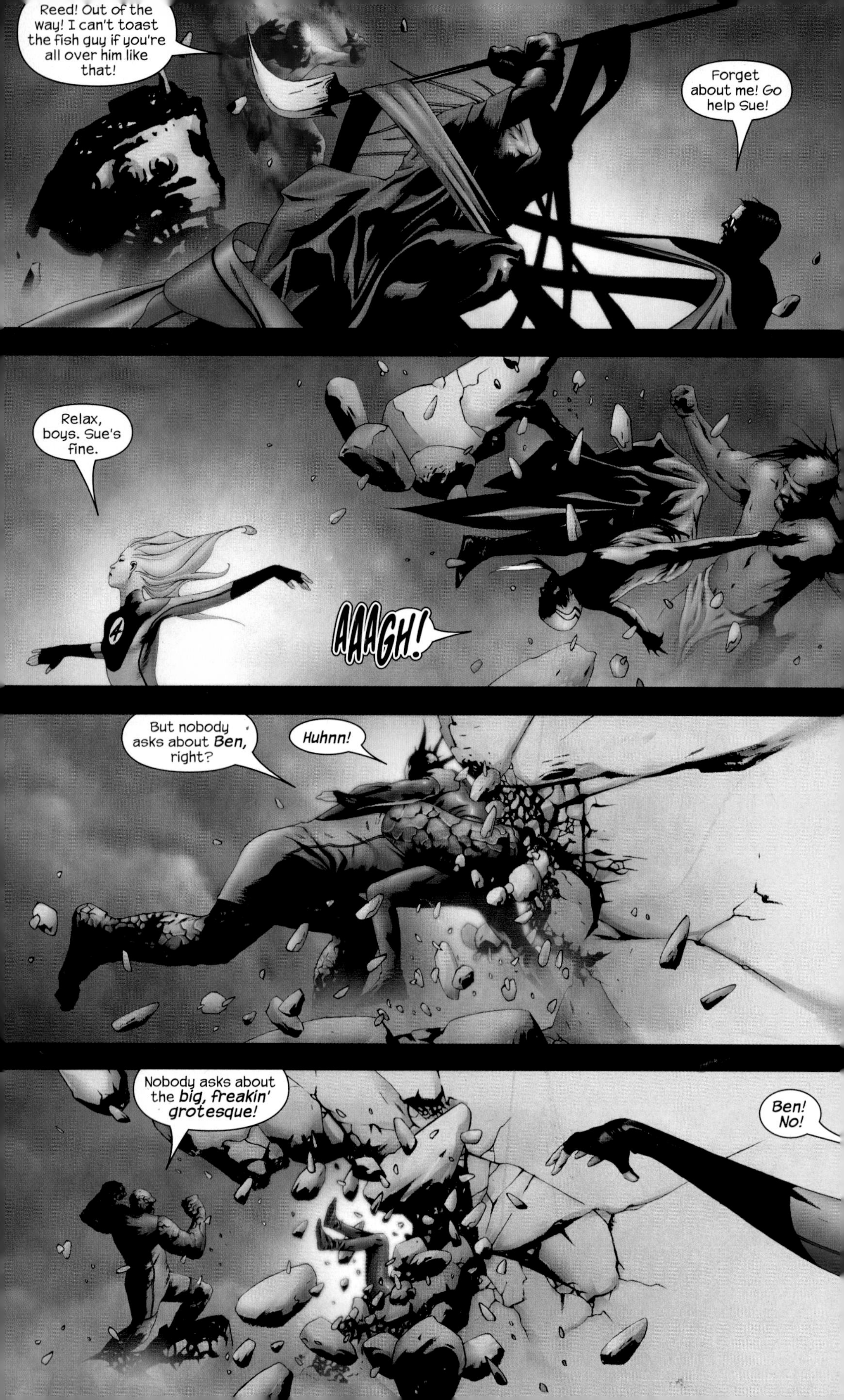
Reed! Out of the way! I can't toast the fish guy if you're all over him like that!
Forget about me! Go help Sue!
Relax, boys. Sue's fine.
AAAGH!
But nobody asks about Ben, right?
Huhnn!
Nobody asks about the big, freakin' grotesque!
Ben! No!

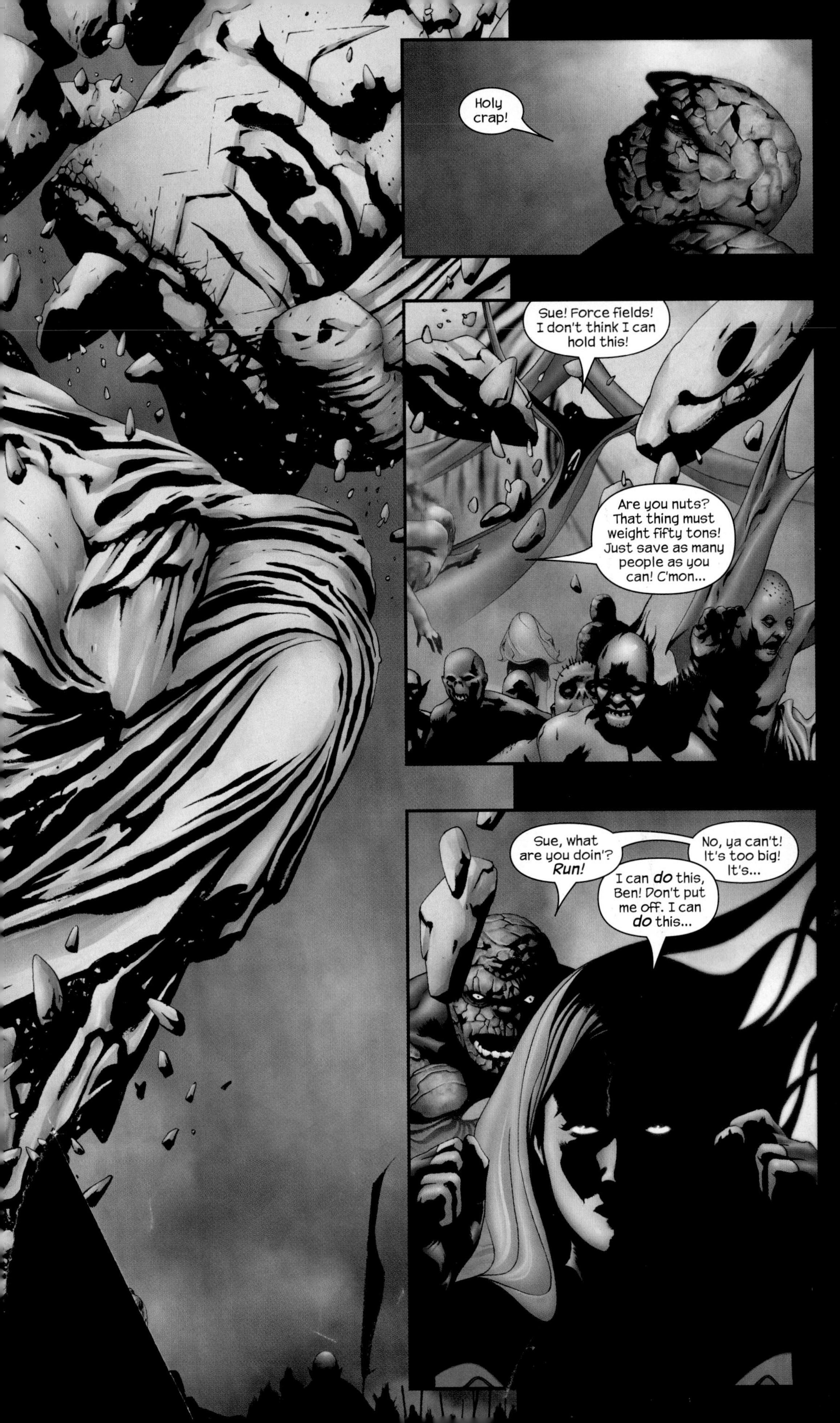
Holy crap!
Sue! Force fields! I don't think I can hold this!
Are you nuts? That thing must weight fifty tons! Just save as many people as you can! C'mon...
Sue, what are you doin'? *Run!*
I can *do* this, Ben! Don't put me off. I can *do* this...
No, ya can't! It's too big! It's...

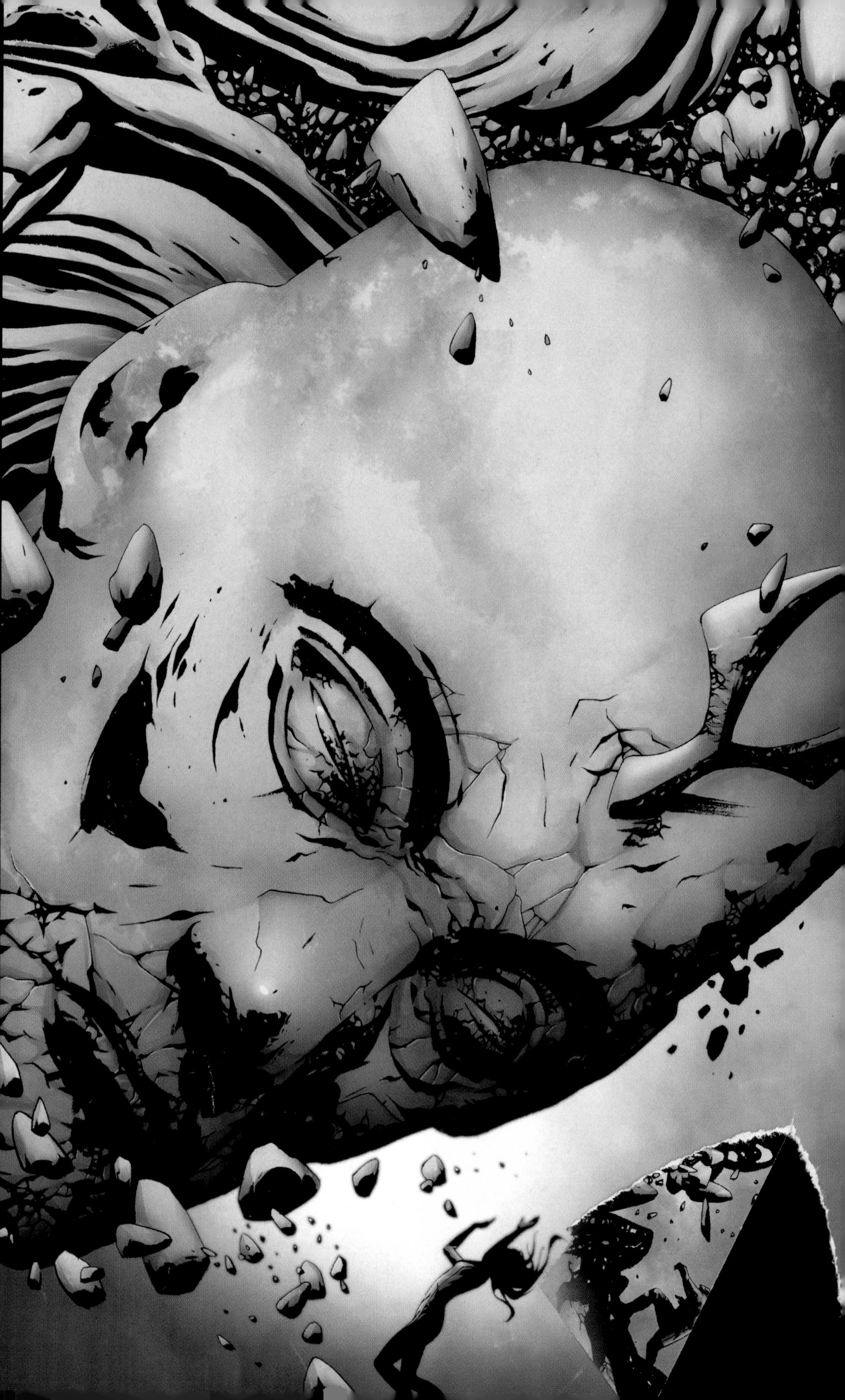

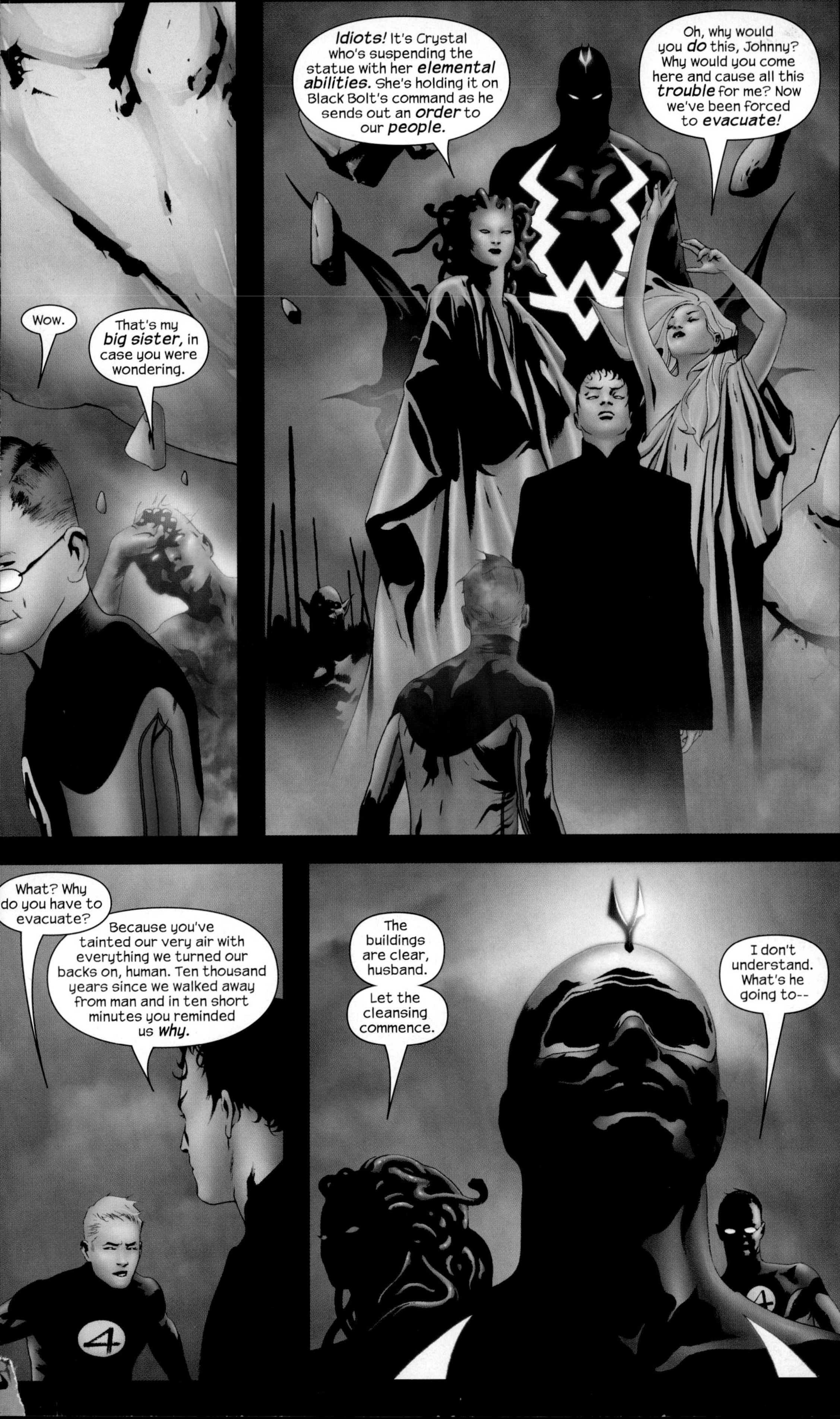
Wow.
That's my big sister, in case you were wondering.
Idiots! It's Crystal who's suspending the statue with her elemental abilities. She's holding it on Black Bolt's command as he sends out an order to our people.
Oh, why would you do this, Johnny? Why would you come here and cause all this trouble for me? Now we've been forced to evacuate!
What? Why do you have to evacuate?
Because you've tainted our very air with everything we turned our backs on, human. Ten thousand years since we walked away from man and in ten short minutes you reminded us why.
The buildings are clear, husband.
Let the cleansing commence.
I don't understand. What's he going to--

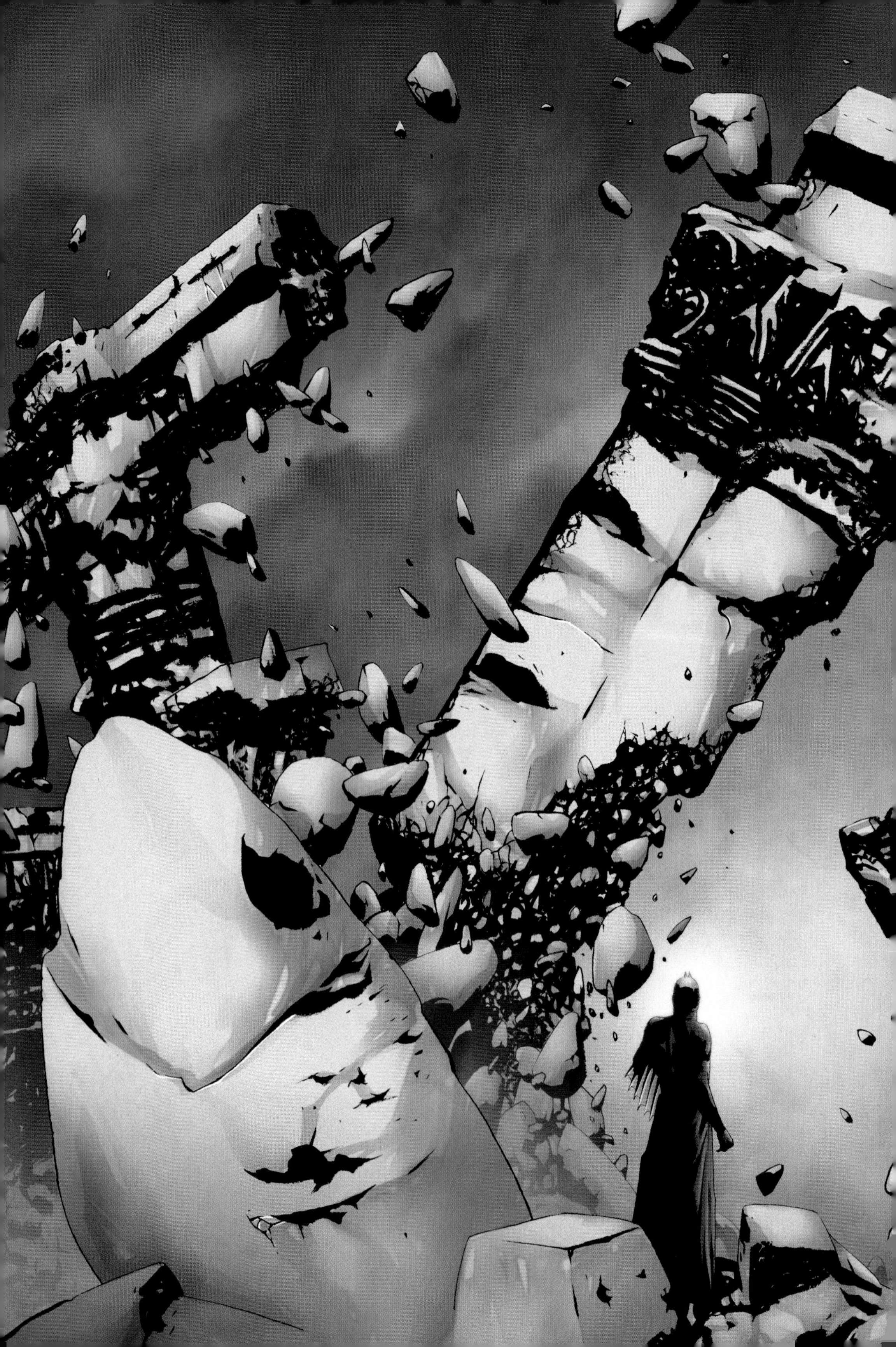

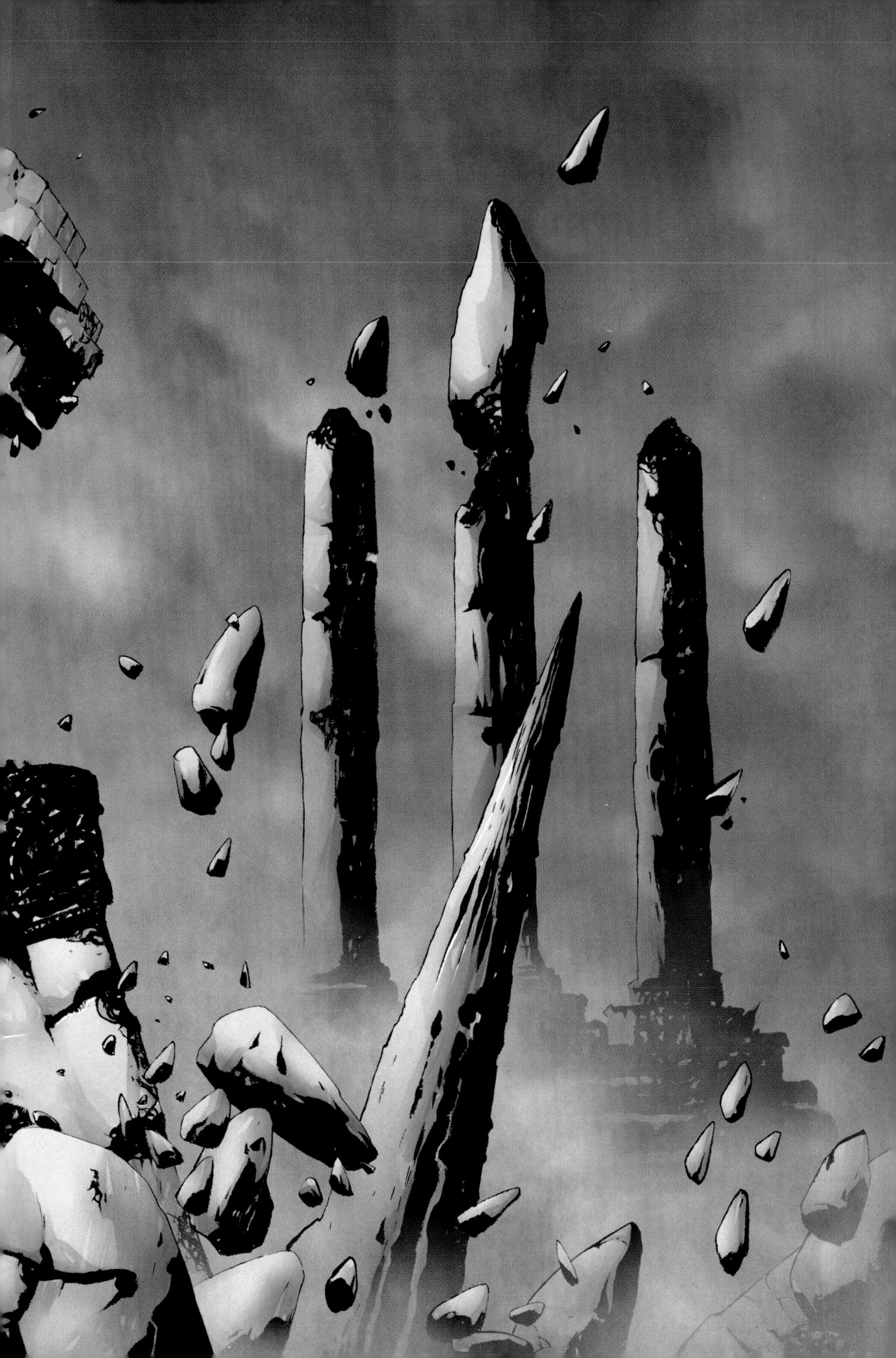

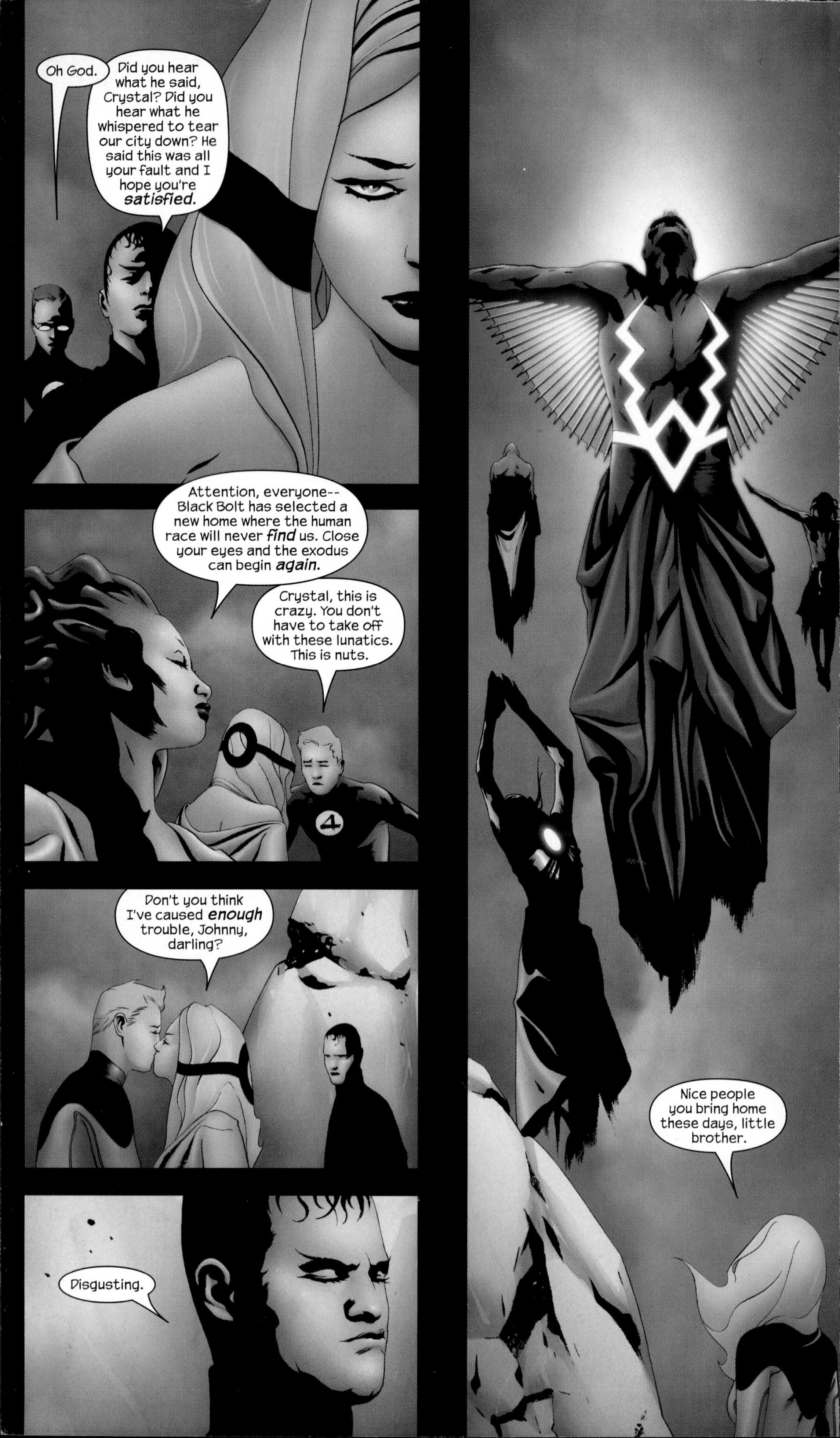
Oh God.
Did you hear what he said, Crystal? Did you hear what he whispered to tear our city down? He said this was all your fault and I hope you're satisfied.
Attention, everyone-- Black Bolt has selected a new home where the human race will never find us. Close your eyes and the exodus can begin again.
Crystal, this is crazy. You don't have to take off with these lunatics. This is nuts.
Don't you think I've caused enough trouble, Johnny, darling?
Disgusting.
Nice people you bring home these days, little brother.

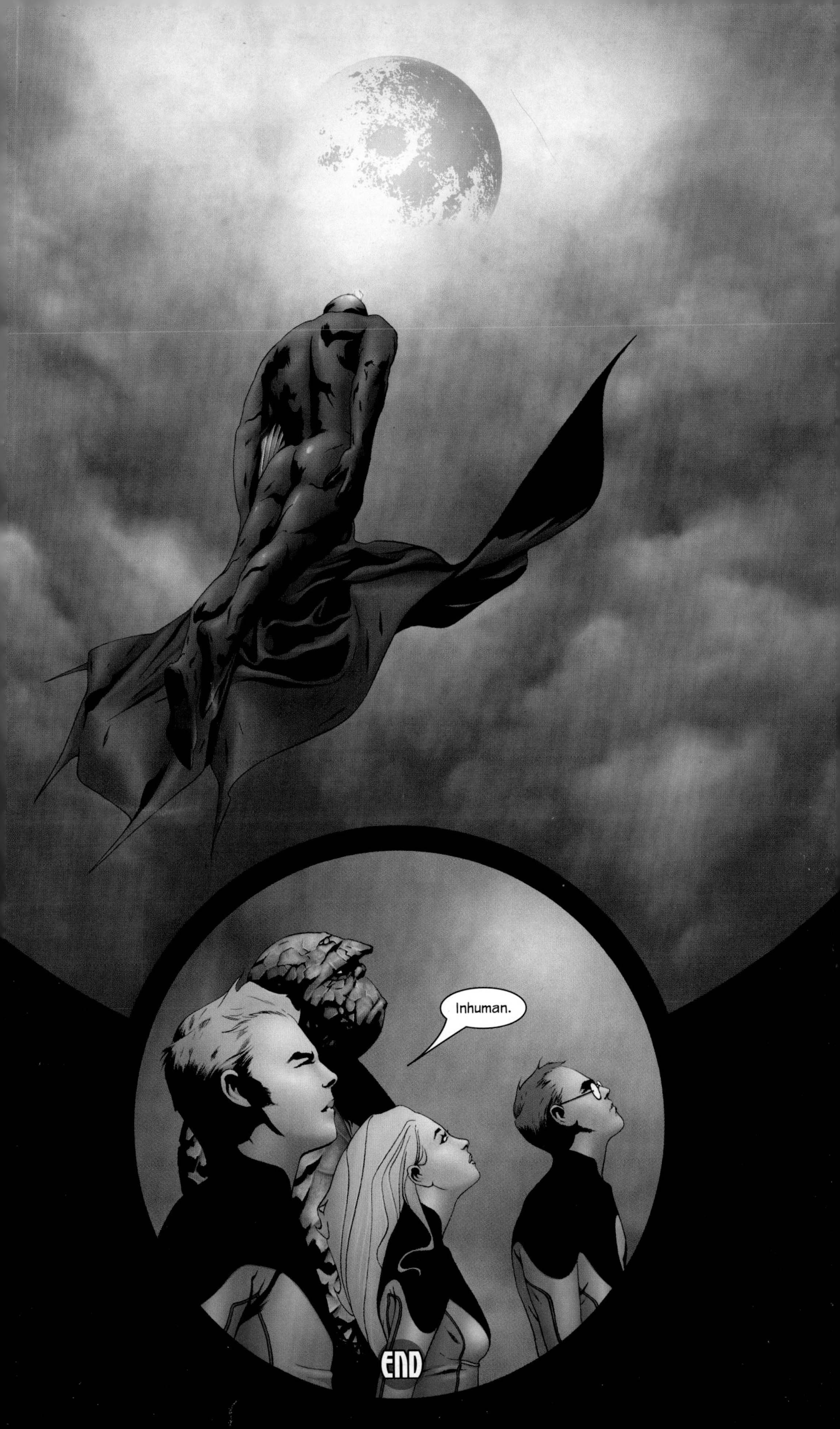
Inhuman.
END

## Character Designs By Jae Lee

### Android

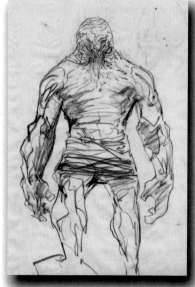

### Gorgon

GORGON

I'M SMARTER THAN YOU.

### Karnak

KARNAK

### The Thinker

IMPLANT DISTORTS HER FACE
I'M SMARTER THAN YOU.
BLACK LEATHER JACKET
THE THINKER

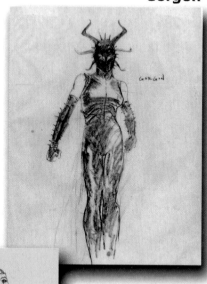

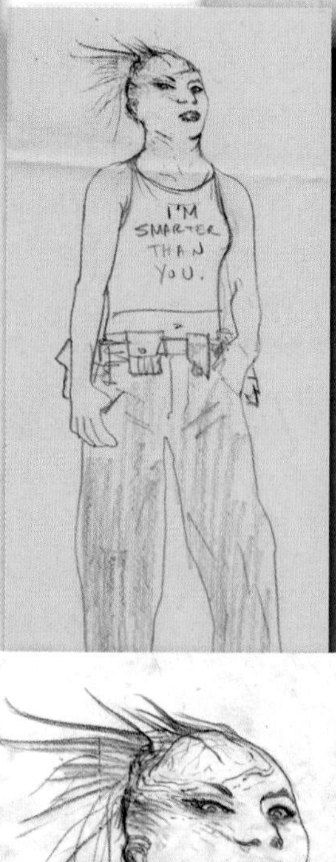

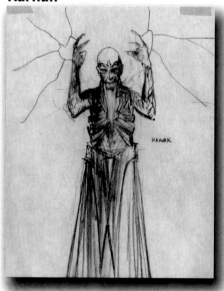

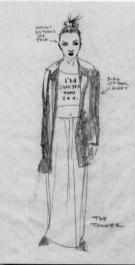

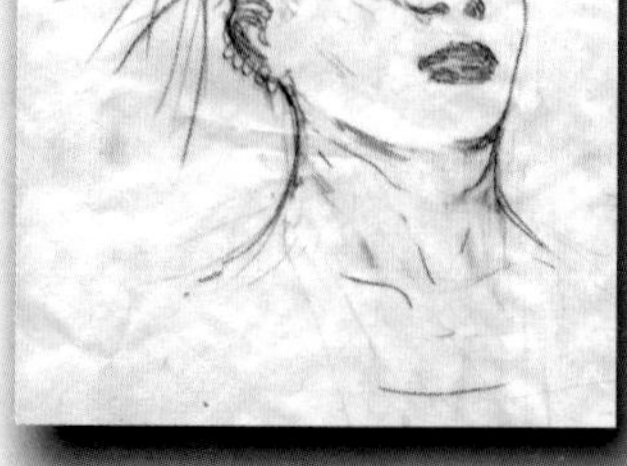